B
LI
NDS
POTS

**Bringing into View
What Christians
are Failing to See**

BLIND SPOTS

Copyright © 2018 Mark J. Musser

Cover art: Image ID : 67321828 – Ion Chiosea

First printing 2018

Printed in the United States of America

Trade paperback ISBN: 9781976825347

Special Thanks To:
God for guiding my steps and for my wife and son
who put up with my missteps

The Hills of Vincere Ridge

Life is anything but easy for fourteen year-old Jason Collins. Adopted and raised by a same-sex couple, his standard school day consists of lingering stares, not-so-subtle whispers, and outright bullying. His only escape, hours of quiet solitude working on his golf swing. Then one weekend, hearing the words of Jesus--Come to me all of you who are weary and carry heavy burdens, and I will give you rest--Jason comes, trusting those words to prove true. Life, however, gets infinitely more difficult. While his moms struggle with his decision to trust Christ, a publicity seeking pastor manipulates the teen into petitioning for new legal guardians, setting off a firestorm of protests, picketing, and media baiting.

Enter TJ Lanter, a former professional golfer still working to overcome his own tragic past. Together, the two use their shared loved of golf to create a bond which enables both to see through their pain and discover that Jesus does indeed embrace the weary and give them rest.

TABLE OF CONTENTS

INTRODUCTION

In an age before driver assist vehicles, I was motoring around an unfamiliar city (Dubuque, Iowa,) and all too quickly became lost. I soon found myself in the far right lane of a four lane thruway scanning street signs in hopes of catching hold of the road I needed.

Suddenly, there it was. To my left and approaching fast.

I quickly glanced in my driver's side view mirror, saw nothing, and turned the wheel hard left. SCREEEEACH! HONK! HONK! HONK! Followed by cursing. Lots and lots of cursing. Not from me, mind you. No, from a black-haired man who clearly did not appreciate my driving skills. He flung open his car door and stormed over to me, as I sat parked on the side of the road trying to figure out how to breathe again.

I honestly did not see him or his car before I attempted my turn. That car, despite its fair size, was completely in my blind spot. Now, could I have looked over my shoulder before turning the wheel? Yes. Should I have? Absolutely. But I didn't. Frankly, had that driver not been so alert, it could have ended far worse.

Today, of course, most new vehicles have blind spot monitoring. Should you try to change lanes or make a turn with a car to your side or rear, a visual or auditory warning is sounded. You then can correct the vehicle...and avoid the cursing. The lots and lots of cursing.

I think the church of American needs something similar.

Indeed, there are blind spots in contemporary Christianity today. Things that we just don't seem to see. Could we turn our head and look? Yes. Should we do so? Absolutely. But, for the most part, we do not. Instead, we content ourselves with quick glances in the side views as we continue headlong on our journey through life in this culture.

I get it. The road is smooth and the seat warmer is soothing. The radio is playing our favorite tunes, and the kids are lost in digital worlds in the back seat. It's clear sailing and steady on. Life is good in the car right now, so why bother with extra effort?

Here's why. Every sixteen year-old with a learner's permit is taught that driving can be dangerous. Sitting behind the wheel of two thousand pounds of machinery, traveling sixty miles an hour, is serious business. We must always be alert. After all, we have our lives to protect, as well as the lives of family, friends, and all those who share the road with us.

The Christian life is no different. Having the only message that can alter the eternal destiny of seven billion people is serious business. Being charged with representing Christ to a world in desperate need of Him is a solemn charge. Because of this, the need to check our blind spots is vital.

Could there be things in those spots that cause our lives to contradict our message, that actually turn people off to God instead of drawing them closer to Him, that hinder or halt the work of the kingdom in our homes, our churches, our communities, and our country? If it is even remotely possible that the answer to any of those questions is "Yes," then we need to do our utmost to monitor these areas and course correct as necessary.

It is my prayer that this book will help us all to turn our heads to see if anything sits hiding in our blind spot.

BLIND SPOT
Sin

In late February 2016, I began prepping for some devotional talks that I would be doing as part of a sports ministry I am involved with. Since Easter was nearing, my thoughts were on the cross and what it signifies.

Thinking on the cross, I was immediately struck by the incredible love of God. What love to sacrifice so much! Truly amazing. Then my thoughts turned to the hope we have because of the cross. Since God defeated sin, death, and the grave, that means He can defeat anything! I can have hope in my struggles and trials and hurts and pain. Because if God can win at the cross, He can win anywhere. Awesome stuff!

Love and hope are indeed incredible topics to think and speak about at Easter, but instead I wanted to speak on something that doesn't get a lot of "air time." Then it hit me. You know what else we see in the cross? We see hate.

Now, before you delete this book from your e-bookshelf and condemn me as a heretic, let me explain. In the cross, we see glorious hope for a great future as well as God's tremendous love for His fallen people, but we also see just how much our heavenly Father *hates* sin.

Since the word *hate* will get a lot of "air-time" in this chapter, it is important that we understand what it means biblically. For instance, since my family is filled with Philadelphia Eagles fans, we often say things like, "I hate the Dallas Cowboys." (This was said too many times to count during the Aikman/Irving/Smith years!) As an impatient driver, I can also be caught saying, "I hate it when people drive 53 in a 55...or even 55 in a 55. Don't people know that 55 means 65?!?"

I am sure you can think of similar instances where you have used this word *hate* to really mean "annoying" or "frustrating." Yet, in the Bible, the word most often used for *hate* can literally be translated as *detestable enmity*.

That is to say, God is not simply annoyed or frustrated by sin. No, He despises sin so much that He has set Himself against it. (Hence the word *enmity* which means *to make an enemy of*.) In short, the Lord cannot stand sin. It is so disgusting and despicable to Him that He has made Himself its enemy. Now, that is something to think about!

There's No Playing with What God Hates

Proverbs 6:16-19 states, *There are six things the Lord hates— no, seven things he detests: haughty eyes, a lying tongue, hands that kill the innocent, a heart that plots evil, feet that race to do wrong, a false witness who pours out lies, a person who sows discord in a family.*

In the Psalms, we read verses like, *Therefore, the proud may not stand in your presence, for you hate all who do evil.*[1] And *the Lord examines both the righteous and the wicked. He hates those who love violence.*[2]

Through the prophet Jeremiah, the Lord laments, *"Again and again I sent my servants, the prophets, to plead with them, 'Don't do these horrible things that I hate so much.'"*[3]

Without a doubt, we see the Lord's hatred for sin throughout both the Old and New Testaments. From Genesis 3 straight through to Revelation, the message is clear. God hates sin. Unfortunately, the contemporary church seems to have a giant blind spot in regards to this and has lost an understanding of what God thinks about sin. Because of this, we tend to think of sin as something we can just choose to ignore or even tolerate.

However, imagine that you were diagnosed with brain cancer. Your family and friends are understandably concerned, and they ask what your next steps are. Incredulously, you respond, "Well, I looked up some cancer jokes on the internet, so I figured I would make some jokes about it and then do my best to ignore it."

Your friends are rightly troubled. "Whoa! If you do that, the cancer will consume you cell by cell until you are dead. You need to begin radical treatment and kill this disease!" They would be correct. The only thing you do with cancer is use every means at your disposal to eradicate it.

Similarly, imagine your home was on fire. As you calmly peer out a window billowing with smoke, you hear the neighbors screaming, "Get out of the house! Get out of the house!"

You wave them off. "Nah, it's no big deal. I'm just gonna tolerate the flames." Again, your neighbors are rightly troubled, for they clearly realize that this conflagration will consume your home plank by plank with you in it. They understand that you must flee the flames, and the fire must be smothered by whatever means necessary.

Just like cancer and fire, the last thing God wants you to do with sin is to think of it as no big deal or to act like you can ignore or tolerate it. The Lord knows very well the devastating effects of sin and how it consumes its victims bit by bit until they are totally corrupted.

In Galatians, the apostle Paul tells us, *Don't be misled—you cannot mock the justice of God. You will **always** harvest what you plant. Those who live only to satisfy their own sinful nature will harvest decay and death from that sinful nature. But those who live to please the Spirit will harvest everlasting life from the Spirit* (emphasis mine).[4]

Wherever there is sin, the result is *always* corruption. There is no "out-clause" for a supposed super-human ability to ignore or tolerate it. In the end, if you believe you can ignore or tolerate sin, either you are lying to you or God is lying to you, (and I think we both know who is doing the lying).

Turning Your Back on Sin
God's Word is abundantly clear. You should never turn a blind eye to sin. Sin cannot be played with, ignored, or tolerated. It always leads to corruption. This is why the Lord hates it. Yes, with a burning passion, He hates sin. It is completely detestable, wholly despicable, and total enmity to Him. Not quite sure if such strong language is warranted? Then consider this:

The doctrine of the Trinity is one of the most amazing aspects of God. Being three distinct persona and, at the same time, one essence is something our finite minds can't quite understand. Nevertheless, Father, Son, and Holy Spirit are so bound in holy love that they are actually joined together in one essence.

Imagine. Since before there was time, the Godhead existed in connected tri-unity. Then Jesus takes on flesh and enters time and space. Even so, in His humanity, He strives to maintain this intimate communion. In the Gospels, we read of Him staying up all night to pray[5] or waking early to spend time with the Father.[6] Even clothed in flesh, Christ still experiences connection and deep union with the Father.

Then the cross...

The Second Member of the Trinity takes our sin upon Himself. Our sin that God truly and totally detests; yes, our sin that God has made His enemy. In His hatred for this sin, God rips Himself from His earthly communion with Christ. Experiencing this disunion for the first time since before there was time, Jesus cries out, "My God, my God, why have you forsaken me?"[7]

Why does God, who had been intimately connected to Christ in this incredible tri-union, rend Himself, turn His back on the incarnate Son, and have Him put to death? Answer: Because God hates sin.

Sin is what makes Hell necessary and is what caused Christ's excruciating sacrifice. If God the Father would tear Himself from Christ because of His incredible hatred for sin, then there are no other options for us. We must hate sin as well. We must stop turning a blind eye to it and see that it is put to death.

Thinking Like Christ
It is very easy to take the world's view of sin—a view that is increasingly tolerant of anything and everything. We, however, can no longer think like the world, nor even trust our own thoughts on the subject. No, we must "have the mind of Christ" and think as He does about sin.

In John 5, after healing a man who had been lame for thirty-eight years, Jesus states, "Now you are well; so stop sinning, or something even worse may happen to you."[8]

In John 8, Jesus encounters a woman caught in adultery. After offering precious forgiveness, He leaves her with this singular instruction, "Go and sin no more."[9]

The Lord inspired Paul to write, *think carefully about what is right, and stop sinning. For to your shame I say that some of you don't know God at all.*[10] And He further inspired John to pen, *everyone who sins is breaking God's law, for all sin is contrary to the law of God. And you know that Jesus came to take away our sins, and there is no sin in him. Anyone who continues to live in him will not sin. But anyone who keeps on sinning does not know him or understand who he is.*[11]

I grew up in a Christian home, thinking I was a pretty good person. After all, I went to church every week, prayed from time to time, and even, every so often, read my Bible outside of church. I mean, come on, if that's not top-tier Christianity for a teenager I don't know what is!

Well, God thought otherwise.

By the time I graduated high school, even I knew I wasn't a "pretty good person" anymore. The mistakes, sins, and irresponsible choices I made are too many to list here, so let's just skip to this -- before I hit age twenty-one, I was a college dropout with very much less than a bright future ahead of me.

Then, just a few weeks before my twenty-first birthday, the Lord literally knocked me to the ground. All at once, my many sins were filing through my brain—a parade of shame and stupidity. Feeling overwhelmed by guilt and humiliation, I wept uncontrollably. It was as though God had stepped into the room, and His holiness was far more than my sinful self could bear.

But suddenly, all at once, a wholly other emotion enveloped me. Love. I do not believe the English language possesses the words to adequately explain the love I felt that day. But I can tell you this, knowing that I was loved so powerfully by a holy God, whom I had offended day after day after day, changed the trajectory of my life.

Think about this now. If you just thought one bad thing a day, said just one inappropriate thing a day, and did just one wrong thing a day, you would still sin over one thousand times each and every year. By the time you hit forty, you would have amassed *at least* 43,800 sins...and that's just from three a day!

Imagine offending someone that many times and yet still be unconditionally loved beyond measure by that person. It's unthinkable, yet that's how it is between God and us. And that realization changed everything for me. I arose from the ground a transformed person.

How could I continue to daily offend someone who loved me so inexpressibly much? Sin was no longer acceptable to me, so I surrendered to the Lord, asked Him to fill me, and begged Him to begin transforming me from the inside out.

How about you? What do you think about your sin? And what do you think about God's unfathomable love for you in spite of it?

No Tolerance Policy
To say my wife hates spiders would be an understatement. Have you seen the meme where charred embers of a burned out house sit above the caption, "Well, what did you expect? I

saw a spider"? That's my wife.

One summer, my wife tagged along with me to a camp where I was teaching Bible classes. I was quite pleased to see that the teachers' cottages were nice and cozy. All that my wife could see, however, were two spider webs dangling in a window sill. She refused to enter the room.

So, with a trusty broom in one hand and a powerful vacuum nozzle in the other, I went through the cottage ridding it of all things spider. When I assured her there was not a single living arachnid left in that room, she finally entered…tentatively.

At home, even though I am not so opposed to spiders (unless they are big and hairy), we keep the local exterminator in business. No eight-legged creature stands a chance in our house, so long as my wife lives there. She makes sure the house is clear of them. There is no corner, crack, or crevice where they can hide!

You might be wondering what my wife's spider policy has to do with what we are talking about. Well, we are to think of sin like my wife thinks of spiders. The Lord has a zero tolerance policy toward all sin and wishes to see it eradicated in every corner, crack, and crevice of our lives. Therefore, our policy must be the same.

What God did with Jesus on that first Good Friday is a stark object lesson for what He expects us to do. As the Son filled with our sin, the Father ripped Himself away and put Jesus to death. In fact, in Isaiah 53, the famous prophecy of Jesus' sacrificial death, we actually read these stunning words, *it was the Lord's **good plan to crush him**…*(emphasis mine)[12]

Crush. It actually says *crush.* The word used in that verse is also used in Scripture to describe grinding things into a fine powder. What a vivid picture! This is what my wife wants to see happen to spiders and what God wants to do with our sin! He wants to pound it into oblivion and see it destroyed. It was His *good plan* to see that done to sin on the cross *and* to see that done to sin in our lives as well.

Colossians 3:5-8 declares, **put to death** *the sinful, earthly things lurking within you. Have nothing to do with sexual immorality, impurity, lust, and evil desires. Don't be greedy, for a greedy person is an idolater, worshiping the things of this world. Because of these sins, the anger of God is coming. You used to do these things when your life was still part of this world. But now is the time to get rid of anger, rage, malicious behavior, slander, and dirty language* (emphasis mine).

In the original Greek, the word used for *put to death* literally means "to kill or to slay." That is our command. Kill the sin in our lives. No longer allow it to live.

I think *The Message* version of the Bible makes the point even clearer. Look at how it translates the above passage. *That means killing off everything connected with that way of death: sexual promiscuity, impurity, lust, doing whatever you feel like whenever you feel like it, and grabbing whatever attracts your fancy. That's a life shaped by things and feelings instead of by God. It's because of this kind of thing that God is about to explode in anger. It wasn't long ago that you were doing all that stuff and not knowing any better. But you know better now, so make sure it's all gone for good: bad temper, irritability, meanness, profanity, dirty talk.*

Think through the movies, TV shows, music, web videos, and video games that you engage in. Think through the magazines you peruse and the books you read. Think through your thought life and your attitudes throughout the day. Are these governed by God's Word or by *doing whatever you feel like whenever you feel like it, and grabbing whatever attracts your fancy?*

Is your sin being starved and put to death or getting three square meals a day and thriving quite nicely?

How Much Sin is Too Much Sin?

My son actually has Christian friends who have ridiculed him because he refuses to watch certain movies or TV shows, play certain video games, listen to certain musical groups, etc. These friends are like, "Are you serious? There's only like five or six bad words in that movie. Maybe the Lord's name is misused a couple times, and there's like one sketchy scene. It's no big deal."

What they are really saying is, "There are only like ten things in it that God hates." Let me ask you an important question. How many things must God hate in something before we should rip ourselves away and seek to kill its hold over us?

How much profanity can a show have, or can you use, before God hates it? Fifteen? Or does the Lord passionately despise every use? How many times can you take, or hear taken, the Lord's name in vain before He hates it? Ten? Or is He totally disgusted by every single misuse of His holy name?

How many sexual thoughts can you entertain in your mind, or treat as entertainment on TV, before God hates it? Five? Or does He not tolerate a single solitary instance? How many times can you rudely speak to someone in a day before God hates it? Three? Or is He completely disgusted the first moment of the first time?

The list could go on and on. However, this is the point where many people start shouting, "Legalism! Legalism! Go back to your Pharisees Anonymous meeting Mark and find healing!"

Please understand. Being in a relationship with the God of the universe through Jesus Christ and then living in obedience to His Word is *not* legalism—it's Christianity.

Jesus clears this up for us in Luke 6. *"Why do you keep calling me 'Lord, Lord!' when you don't do what I say? I will show you what it's like when someone comes to me, listens to my teaching, and then follows it. It is like a person building a house who digs deep and lays the foundation on solid rock. When the floodwaters rise and break against that house, it stands firm because it is well built. But anyone who hears and doesn't obey is like a person who builds a house right on the ground, without a foundation. When the floods sweep down against that house, it will collapse into a heap of ruins."*[13]

In the Gospel of John, Jesus also makes His expectations abundantly plain when He says things like, *"If you love me, you will obey my commands."*[14]

"You are my friends, when you do what I command."[15]

"All who love me will do what I say. My Father will love them, and we will come and make our home with each of them. Anyone who doesn't love me will not obey me."[16]

To avoid anything in this book being construed as legalism, I have loaded it with Scriptural truth. Yet, still let me say this. If you find anything in this book that isn't backed by the Bible, then you can chuck it. In fact, you should most definitely chuck it. You will not find much to chuck, though; because God's Word is plain. He has a zero tolerance policy for the things He hates—like profanity, the misusage of His name, anything beyond a hint of sexual immorality, disrespect of authority, etc.

Doing whatever you feel like whenever you feel like it and grabbing whatever attracts your fancy and then claiming "legalism" when someone confronts you in your sin may make you feel better, but it's not fooling God.

To Know Love You Must Understand Hate

Please realize that God deeply loves us beyond all possible measure, but He also has an equally deep and passionate hatred for the sin we so easily turn a blind eye to. In fact, I don't think you can really grasp the depths of the Father's love for you until you truly embrace His intolerable hatred for sin.

We constantly do things, think things, and treat things as entertainment that God finds rightly disgusting and detestable, yet He still loves us anyway! Sadly, as our culture has lost God's hatred for sin in its blind spot, we have also lost sight of how amazing His love and grace really is.

In 1773, John Newton penned the most famous hymn in history *Amazing Grace.* The first line of that classic song boldly announces, "Amazing Grace, how sweet the sound, that saved a *wretch* like me" (Emphasis mine). How many in our modern American culture would actually think themselves *wretched* in God's sight? So few, in fact, that some modern hymnals have changed the word *wretch* to *man.*

In 1738, Charles Wesley penned my favorite hymn *And Can it Be* as a celebration of his conversion that same year. The first stanza reads:

And can it be that I should gain
An interest in the Savior's blood?
Died He for me, who caused His pain—
For me, who Him to death pursued?
Amazing love! How can it be,

That Thou, my God, shouldst die for me?

In a time when an understanding of sin's evil was more prevalent, we read of God's "amazing grace" and His "amazing love." Both John Newton and Charles Wesley understood the depths of their depravity and were overwhelmed that God would love them anyway. Even more, that He would come and die in their places for their abhorrent transgressions.

While I love much of contemporary Christian music today, I often joke that I need to start carrying insulin around with me because so much of today's Christian music is filled with such sugary fluff that listening too long just might send me into a diabetic coma!

Today's Christian music is woefully one-sided. We are often reminded of God's incredible love and grace (which are important things to be reminded of). Yet, we cannot fully comprehend the "incredibleness" of that love and grace because we hear nothing of the Lord's unsurpassed holiness nor His passionate hatred for the sin we so readily commit.

Nevertheless, while contemporary Christian music, and even contemporary Christianity, would like to keep our sin problem in a blind spot, God does not ignore it so we cannot either. We must seek to kill the desire for it in our lives through the power of the Holy Spirit inside us. This means turning the channel, leaving the theater, not buying the video game, clicking off the website, shutting down the thought, curbing the attitude, standing biblically on present-day matters like abortion, same-sex unions, transgender issues, and more.

The Pathway to Grieving the Lord
Proverbs 8:13 says, *All who fear the Lord will hate evil.*

Moreover, Romans 12:9 instructs us to *hate what is evil and cling tightly to what is good.*

When we do not strive to do this, it only leads one direction. Away from God. It has been said what one generation allows in moderation, the next allows in excess. John Wesley put it this way. "What one generation tolerates, the next generation embraces." This is true in our culture, and it is also true in our lives.

Bit by bit as corruption sets in, standards erode in our lives, and we start to become something wholly other than God intended when He made a way for salvation through Christ. Suddenly, we have multitudes of Christians seeing movies like *Deadpool* and *Fifty Shades of Grey* then talking, tweeting, and posting about how great they are. We have Christian parents buying video games like *Grand Theft Auto V* for their children. Pornography overruns Christian homes, and churches celebrate the Supreme Court decision to uphold same-sex marriage by placing "Love Wins" on their street-side display boards.

How this must anger the Lord. But worse than angering Him, how it must grieve His holy heart. Why do I think grieving God is worse than angering Him, you ask? Keep reading.

I remember when my son was fourteen. For the previous six months, he had been headlong into sin and denial. I could see how his choices were affecting his life, and how they would continue to affect his life for years to come. Yet, he seemed oblivious to it.

After one particularly bad day, I sat with him at our dining room table. As I laid out the last six months, emotion overcame me. I bawled harder than perhaps I ever had before. I was totally anguished and overwhelmed by how his choices were affecting him.

I think everyone with children would agree with me when I say this. As a parent, I would much prefer to be angry at my child than to be grieved by his life-choices. There have been times when my son, Kyle, really got me fuming, and we joke about some of those things now. But when I think of crying with Kyle at my dining room table, I feel bad even now. It wasn't funny then, and it never will be.

The Bible says that when we sin, when we engage in what God hates by watching it, playing with it, buying movie tickets to see it, surfing it on the web, He is grieved. In Genesis 6, we read these words, *the Lord observed the extent of human wickedness on the earth, and he saw that everything they thought or imagined was consistently and totally evil. So the Lord was sorry he had ever made them and put them on the earth. It broke his heart.*[17]

Ephesians 4:30 states, *do not bring sorrow to God's Holy Spirit by the way you live.* The word used for sorrow in that verse literally means "pain or anguish." In other words when we engage in sin, which leads us down a path of corruption, it brings pain and anguish to the Father. He weeps and grieves over what we are becoming--individually and as a culture.

Frankly, thinking about all of this reminds me of the time I carelessly turned left in Dubuque! How could I have missed something as big as a car? Easy. It was lost in my blind spot. Has sin been lost in yours? If so, what course correction will you make?

BLIND SPOT
Gossip

There's a story of four preachers who met regularly for a friendly gathering. During conversation one day, the shortest of the preachers said, "Our people come to us and pour out their hearts, confess certain sins and needs. Let's do the same. Confession is good for the soul." All agreed.

One confessed he liked to go to the race track/casino and would sneak off to those places when away from his church. The second confessed to smoking cigars, while the third opened up about using foul language when angry. When it came to the fourth one, however; he wouldn't share a thing. Finally, the others pressed him saying, "Come on, we confessed ours. What is your secret vice?"

To that he answered, "It's gossiping, and I can hardly wait to get out of here!"[1]

All joking aside (if you call that a joke), I think the two biggest gossip centers on the planet are churches and small towns. And since I pastored a church in a small town for five years, I think I am uniquely qualified to speak on the blind spot of gossip.

Welcome to Belmont – Population 871

Tucked near the southwest corner of Wisconsin is the picturesque little town of Belmont. It was once the capital of "Wisconsin Territory," but that was a loooong time ago. When I pastored there, the population was 871. Not bad for a town in Lafayette County which, when I was there, was noted for two things: Having more cows than people and not having a single traffic light.

My family and I didn't live in the town of Belmont itself. Our house was actually three miles down the road. We had exactly three neighbors, a fact that made trick-or-treating really fun for our son! Go to three houses, get a pack of M&M's, a caramel apple, and some lint…night over.

Meanwhile, a traffic jam in Belmont usually involved two tractors and a combine moving from one field to another or some cows loose and hanging out in the middle of road. Traffic reports weren't done by helicopter. A local farmer would climb his silo and call the sheriff on his cellphone. You think I'm making that up, don't you? Oh, but I'm not. It actually happened once. This is life in a small town.

Of course, what's also true about small towns is that everyone knows everyone else. When I walked into the bank for the first time, having been in town for less than a week, I was greeted by name. They knew who I was because I was the only new guy. I'd walk into my son's school, kindergarten through twelfth grade all in one building, and people I'd never seen before in my life would greet me with "Hey, Pastor Mark."

And you are…?

But here's the thing about small towns, people will give you the shirt off their back and do anything for you. When my son was in second or third grade, he wanted to take Hot Pockets to school for lunch. I told him that he couldn't because they needed to be microwaved first. He insisted the cafeteria staff would accommodate. Immediately, my mind flashed back to my own time as an elementary school student and wondered what would have happened had I asked a lunch lady to heat up a Hot Pocket for me. My brain only could imagine incessant laughter coming from behind a metal counter! Sure enough, though, I asked the cafeteria staff at my son's school and was told, "Sure, no problem!"

Another time, when the school bus broke down, the driver went door to door picking up the kids in his car! Since everyone in the town knew the bus driver, no one had a problem with that sort of thing. Hey, you don't get that kind of service in suburbia!

In these ways, small towns are *very much* like churches. In most churches, everyone knows everyone else. Further, in most churches, members will step up and meet any need a fellow church member may have. These things definitely are what make many small towns and many churches fantastic.

However, in small towns, there is certainly a bad side to everyone knowing everyone else--that is, everyone wants to talk about everyone else's business. Moreover, if you are a more prominent person in a small town like one of just three pastors, or one of just thirteen teachers, or one of the two police officers in Belmont, you would find your business talked about more than others.

Unfortunately, it is like that in churches as well, where there is more than a fair share of gossip. And, if you feel called to head a ministry or head a church, you will almost assuredly face more gossip than most.

Of course, some will say, "Well, it's just words." Those

people, however, fail to recognize the sheer power of the spoken word…until it is too late. This is why the blind spot of gossip has ruined more than its share of friendships, families, and church fellowships. It's time to adjust our side views again and bring this huge problem into our field of vision.

Living, Breathing Words

Proverbs 18:21 candidly states that *the tongue can bring death or life; those who love to talk will reap the consequences.*

The original language of this verse is Hebrew. In the Hebrew mindset, when you spoke a word, you actually created a living thing. Just as God brought life and creation into existence through His word, so the Hebrews believed that when your breath pushed words past your lips, life came forth. And, sometimes, that life caused death to the listener.

Understand, God's words created the universe and brought life to this planet. Since we are made in His image, this means our words also have great power--power to encourage, to bless, to give life, and also to curse, to crush, and to kill.

Idiot! Moron! You fool!

I love you! Way to go! Great job!

You do not need to see me for those words to have an effect. Without me being present, my words still exist, my words still, right now, are causing you to think, to ponder, to wonder. Make no mistake. Words have virtually unlimited power.

Words can hurt. Words can heal. Words can uplift. Words can bring down. Words can bless people and bless a church. Words can kill people and kill a church. You may have heard the expression, "Sticks and stones may break my bones, but words will never hurt me" which is one of the dumbest sayings ever recorded. It's right up there with Joe Theismann saying, "Nobody in football should be called a genius. A genius is a guy like Norman Einstein."[2]

If I struck you with a stone, you would have instant pain and then a bruise for a few days. But if I belittled you in front of everyone you love, the pain of my words could burn in your heart for twenty years or more. In fact, you might never get over it.

When I was teen, there were about thirty kids in the youth ministry I attended. Out of those thirty, I was *the last* person anyone ever expected to grow up and be a pastor. I am not exaggerating. In fact, if someone had come to my church when I was a teen and said, "Mark will grow up to be a pastor," he would have been condemned as a heretic and beaten out of the church with broomsticks!

You know what? When you have that kind of reputation, even if you didn't do the bad thing, everyone still thinks you did. The gossip goes around, and thirty years later, as I type this, it's just as hurtful as it was then. When I see those who gossiped about me three decades ago, it's the first thing I think about--their words, their lies, and their gossip. It all comes flooding back.

True, sticks and stones may break your bones, but words can crush your spirit.

The Power of the Tongue
The Bible says, in Proverbs 15:4, *gentle words bring life and health; a deceitful tongue crushes the spirit.*

Look again at Proverbs 18, this time with a bit more context.

Wise words satisfy like a good meal; the right words bring satisfaction. The tongue can bring death or life; those who love to talk will reap the consequences.[3]

Everything you say is alive and bears fruit, and that fruit either satisfies and blesses the hearer or leaves a person feeling empty and hollow. Now, let's look at one more Scripture. Perhaps the most famous one regarding the power of the tongue.

Dear brothers and sisters, not many of you should become teachers in the church, for we who teach will be judged more strictly. Indeed, we all make many mistakes. For if we could control our tongues, we would be perfect and could also control ourselves in every other way. We can make a large horse go wherever we want by means of a small bit in its mouth. And a small rudder makes a huge ship turn wherever the pilot chooses to go, even though the winds are strong. In the same way, the tongue is a small thing that makes grand speeches. But a tiny spark can set a great forest on fire. And among all the parts of the body, the tongue is a flame of fire. It is a whole world of wickedness, corrupting your entire body. It can set your whole life on fire, for it is set on fire by hell itself.[4]

That Scripture paints a vivid picture, doesn't it? The tongue as a blazing flame of destruction set on fire by Hell itself. Totally graphic…and a wake-up call for all of us who are loose with our words. Just as one spark can start a fire that destroys a forest, so one careless word or bit of gossip can begin the process of destroying a person, a marriage, a friendship, a family, or a church.

This is the power of words. This is the power of the tongue. It's certainly way too much power to leave hiding in your blind spot. Studies show that children who deal with an overabundance of negative words are more at risk to suffer from a host of behavioral and emotional issues. In regards to marriage, a University of Denver study tracked couples for their first ten years of marriage and found that couples that divorced within that ten year period used two to five times as many negative words with each other than those couples that stayed married.[5] And when it comes to churches, how many people have left a church, or how many churches have split, over the power of words?

That being the case, we need to ask ourselves a couple of very important questions: What kind of words do I use, and what are the effects of those words? I suggest pausing a few moments and thinking that through before moving on.

Wait? Gossip is Equal to What?

Take a look at what Paul writes in Romans 1:29-32. *Their lives became full of every kind of wickedness, sin, greed, hate, envy, murder, quarreling, deception, malicious behavior, and gossip. They are backstabbers, haters of God, insolent, proud, and boastful. They invent new ways of sinning, and they disobey their parents. They refuse to understand, break their promises, are heartless, and have no mercy. They know God's justice requires that those who do these things deserve to die, yet they do them anyway. Worse yet, they encourage others to do them, too.*

Wow! There's some words with the power to punch you right in the gut! How'd you like to have the Apostle Paul over to speak at a dinner party? Talk about bringing lead balloons to a parade.

But, in those verses, did you happen to catch something, something right in the same list with murder, being a hater of God, and heartless? Right along with those terrible things is

27

gossip. Whoa! Think about this now. Paul says those people's lives were filled with every kind of wickedness and evil, and then he starts listing all that is wicked and evil. Smack in the middle of that list of wicked and evil things is gossip!

So that means when we gossip, it is no little thing. Quite the opposite in fact, for the Bible says it's *wicked and evil.* It's a killer and a destroyer. And, on top of all of that, the Scripture also starkly announces that *those who do these things deserve to die.* Forget about a lead balloon. That's poo in the punchbowl!

Maybe, just maybe, gossip is a way bigger issue than we think it is.

Of course, Satan loves to trick us into thinking we are doing people a favor when we talk about them. Like when we make "a prayer request" for someone, or talk about a situation like we are concerned, when really we just want to share the dirt. Well, Satan might enjoy such things, but the Lord is most definitely not a fan. (Remember chapter 1?) It's clear from His Word that He would have us adjust our side view mirrors again to get the scourge of gossip plainly into sight.

Secret Slandering and Scandal Mongering
In the original language of the New Testament, Greek, the word for *gossip* in Romans 1 literally means *whisper lies* or *slander in secret.* Frankly, we often try to put a positive spin on gossip, but the Bible doesn't really give us that option. I am pretty sure there is no way to put a positive spin on whispering lies or slandering in secret, regardless of what we say our motive is.

Now, get this. If you think the New Testament puts a bad spin on gossip, the Hebrew word in the Old Testament literally means *scandal monger* or *merchant of tales*. Again, there is no use for even a politician to attempt a positive spin on that! (I think many would give it a go though.)

It is just sin, pure and simple. A sin that can separate friends, ruin families, crush church leaders, and split a church. Look again at the book of Proverbs. In chapter sixteen, we read, *Scoundrels create trouble; their words are a destructive blaze. A troublemaker plants seeds of strife; gossip separates the best of friends.*[6]

Here we see again that words like scoundrel, trouble, troublemaker, strife, destruction, and gossip are all linked together. Truly, nothing good comes from gossip. Nothing at all. And while gossip tends to be stereotyped as a woman's issue, it is an equal opportunity offender for both males and females.

Back to Belmont
Let me take you back to quaint Belmont, Wisconsin where I had a gossipy couple in my church, and, ooooh, the problems they caused! I prayed and prayed about this and finally decided that I needed to confront this pair. Before I did, though, I called all their previous pastors that I could find and was able to track down every one, all the way back to the early 1970s, basically to the time I was born!

In fact, I would call a pastor and start the conversation with, "Listen, I have a couple in the church that is causing some problems, and they were in the church with you, so I…" The pastor on the other end would cut me off and say, "Can I guess who it is? Is it _____?" They were right!

A few days later, I set up a meeting and took along four decades of evidence and a trusted layman in the church. The four of us sat down together, and I laid it all out, finishing with, "You need to stop it or you need to leave." They promised they would stop, go home, pray, and yada, yada, yada.

Well, I don't know what they prayed, but it got *twice* as bad. Their gossip flooded through the small town like a dam break. Frankly, life is just too short for all of that, so my family and I left the church. Of course, I am sure that couple thought they had won themselves a nice little battle, but no one wins when gossip is rife.

Within a short while, church attendance was cut by over fifty percent. Several families left, and the church could only afford to have a pastor come in on Sundays. The power of words.

Gossip is just as cruel a killer as cancer. Perhaps even more so, because no one invites cancer in. Yet, how many of us invite gossip in? Satan loves to fill us with a, "Guess what I know attitude." As it says in Proverbs 26, *rumors are dainty morsels that sink deep into one's heart.*[7]

The devil wants us to feel like we need to be in the know about everyone. We need to be an insider and get the scoop. But really we are just scandal mongering and selling stories. Really we are just whispering lies and secretly slandering. Really, it is just as wicked and evil as murder, hate, and rebellion. There's no positively spinning that.

Are You Building Up or Tearing Down?
Proverbs 11:11 reads, *upright citizens are good for a city and make it prosper, but the talk of the wicked tears it apart.* That verse has plenty of meat already, but allow me to change a couple words, then let's read this again. *Upright congregants are good for a church and make it prosper, but the talk of the wicked tears it apart.*

Think about that verse and ask yourself, "Are my words blessing the church or tearing it apart? When I speak about the music of the church, am I creating a division between those who like hymns and those who like choruses, or am I praising those who are using their gifts to serve God in music?"

"When I talk about the pastors, am I creating a division between those who like the direction of the church and those who don't, or am I praising leaders who are trying to follow God's will?"

"When I talk about certain ministries in the church, am I creating division between those who like a certain ministry and those who don't, or am I blessing those who are striving to serve God as they believe He is calling them?"

What are your words doing in your family, in your marriage, in your workplace, and in your church? Are they blessing and building, or are they tearing down? If you are blessing and building, don't stop! If you are tearing apart, please stop!

Before we move on to the next blind spot, let's look at three quick things that can help us evaluate whether or not we should be speaking about someone or something.

ONE -- As my mother used to tell me, if you don't have anything nice to say, don't say anything at all. That is a good thing to keep in mind when tempted to gossip. If it's not good and uplifting, don't share it with another. If you have something constructive or corrective that needs to be said, then it should be said only to the person who needs to hear it, not to others.

TWO -- Realize that if you are not speaking directly to someone who is part of the problem or you have *not* been asked to be part of the solution, then you should not be talking about it. In Matthew 18:15-17, Jesus very clearly directs us to go to the person you have issue with. You are simply being unbiblical and causing more harm than good if you do otherwise.

THREE --Think before you speak. Before saying anything, ask yourself: Is it true? It is helpful? Is it inspiring? Is it necessary? Is it kind?

Finally, let me leave you with wise words found in Ephesians 4:29, *do not let any unwholesome talk come out of your mouths, but only what is helpful for building others up according to their needs, that it may benefit those who listen.*

BLIND SPOT
The Fear of the Lord

"You just wait until your father gets home!"

The above eight words are ones no child wants to hear from his or her mom. Yet, I must confess, my sister and I heard that unwanted octet more times than we cared to. After those words came flying angrily out of Mom's mouth, we were marched off to our bedrooms to await our fate. Since my sister's room faced the front of the house, she would anxiously peer out her window and whisper a play by play across the hall to me.

"Car's coming." Hold breath through an uncomfortable pause. "It's not Dad."

Breathe again.

Sadly, it would always end with, "Car's coming…it's Dad." Shortly thereafter, the creak of the front door, muffled voices in the kitchen, the pounding of dress shoes up the steps, followed by "unpleasantness."

Indeed, knowing that we had done wrong and were deserving of consequences, my sister and I waited fearfully for Dad to come home. But let me be clear. We did not fear my father, just the consequences he would be bringing.

Most days, I waited excitedly for my father to come home. You could find me many an evening pacing the front porch with a baseball glove or a Wiffleball bat in hand. I didn't even give Dad time to put down his briefcase or change his shoes before I asked, "Are you ready to play?"

Time for Some Healthy Fear
Sadly, as many Americans drive down the road of life, a healthy fear of the Lord is lost in their blind spot. If "the fear of the Lord" does come to mind, it is usually equated with a frightened child hiding under a bed as his father's drunken footsteps draw near. Such a thought, however, is nowhere near the truth.

To fear the Lord does not mean to dread Him or His presence. Never! We should long for God's presence, as I longed for my father to come home so we could play baseball. What the fear of the Lord actually refers to is understanding that He is the one in charge. When we make sinful choices that go against His will, He *will* answer with consequences—sometimes quite unpleasant ones.

Studies show that children who have a healthy fear of their parents grow up to be the most well-adjusted. A Pathways to Desistance study found that teens who described their parents as "warm and firm" were more mature, more academically competent, less prone to internalize distress and less likely to engage in risky behavior than their peers.

In regards to this, an article in the *Temple Review* stated, "The study lends some support to the contention that especially firm parenting...may be more beneficial to youth, protecting them from harm."[1]

In discussing another study from the University of Minnesota, speaker and author Chip Ingram writes, "The balanced, authoritative parent who combines high levels of support with high levels of control typically produced children with high self-esteem, good coping skills, and a positive relationship with parents."[2]

Certainly, recent research shows that children who know their parents love them, yet also understand that doing wrong means consequences, are going to make the best adults. Conversely, these same studies show that parents who are "high love" but "low discipline" create feelings of low self-esteem and inferiority in their children.[3]

The reason? Children with little to no boundaries are always questioning themselves. They never know for sure what is right or wrong, safe or not safe. With no clear boundaries, their seeming freedom only leads to insecurity and doubt. And without discipline, they never learn responsibility.

Underscoring this, a study by Brigham Young University found that teens of indulgent parents were three times more likely to make irresponsible choices..."[4] This is because, writes author, professor, and psychologist John Santrock, "children [of indulgent parents] never learn to control their own behavior and always expect to get their way."[5]

The evidence is clear. High love coupled with high discipline is the best combination a parent can use to raise healthy and well-adjusted children who will work hard, serve faithfully, and effectively raise children of their own. (For more on this, see my book *The Christ-Centered Home*.)

Yet, when it comes to Father God, our culture seems to view

Him as an indulgent parent who has lost the "high discipline" and only engages in "high love." Because of this, we've become like the children of indulgent parents making irresponsible choices, never learning to control our behavior, and always expecting to get our own way without any thought that God may be displeased with us.

Grace Always Wins…Huh?

As I type these words, there is a song I've heard on the radio quite a bit. The bridge goes something like this...*For the prodigal son, grace wins… For the woman at the well, grace wins… For the blind man and the beggar, grace wins… For always and forever, grace wins… Singing hallelujah, grace wins every time. Every time.*[6]

Since these lyrics are put to a catchy tune, one can quite easily find him or herself singing right along. I know I did...but then I started to think about the words. Grace wins every time? Is that really, and biblically, true?

What about Moses begging the Lord to allow him into the Promised Land? God's response? "That's enough! Speak of it no more!" and the prophet was denied entry. (See Deuteronomy 3:23-29) That doesn't sound like grace wins every time.

What about Achan, who took what was forbidden from Jericho? God's response? He told Joshua to condemn Achan, and his entire family, to death. (See Joshua 7:19-26.) Again, is that an example of grace wins every time?

Then there is King David. He committed adultery with Bathsheba and killed her husband, Uriah, as part of a half-baked cover up. Though David pleaded for forgiveness, and was forgiven, the son born of his union with Bathsheba died and the Lord promised that peace would *never* again be part of David's line. (See 2 Samuel 12). Another example of grace wins every time?

You may also consider Ananias and Sapphira in Acts 5. Both struck dead by the Lord after the Apostle Peter confronts them about lying to the church. Think too of Hymenaeus and Alexander. Of them, the Apostle Paul states in 1 Timothy 1:20, *I threw them out and handed them over to Satan so they might learn not to blaspheme God.*

And finally, what about Jesus in the Garden of Gethsemane, pleading with the Father to allow the cup of suffering to pass from Him? In that moment, Christ came to understand that God's justice, not His grace, must win if there were to be any real chance for us to ever experience grace.

Picking and choosing Scriptures to create a theology of God is dangerous. Sure, it is much more pleasant to dwell on, and sing about, God's love and grace, but He is not just full of love and grace. He is also full of truth, justice, and holiness. The same Scriptures that boldly proclaim that *God is love* also proclaim *God is holy.*[7]

You certainly wouldn't want to babysit a kid whose parents only allowed grace to win. "What's that little Johnny? You tried to set the dog on fire? Well, that's alright. Let's go out for some ice-cream."

Any parents that are "grace only" would have kids who are spoiled at best or, at worst, are like the "affluenza teen" who made so many headlines—totally immature and unable to deal with the difficulties of life.

When we say God is grace and love only, we develop a mistaken and misshapen theology--one where God does not demand or require anything of us. One where we can be and do whatever we want to be and do without thought of consequences. However, we cannot base our theology on what the culture thinks or on what singers sing. Our theology has to be based on Scripture--and not just the parts of Scripture that we like. It must be based on all of it.

The Blessing of Fear

Psalm 111:10 states, *fear of the Lord is the foundation of true wisdom.*

In Proverbs 1:7, Solomon writes, *fear of the Lord is the foundation of true knowledge, but fools despise wisdom and discipline.*

Solomon would also go on to note in verse 14:27 that *the fear of the Lord is a life-giving fountain; it offers escape from the snares of death.*

And for those who think the fear of the Lord is just an "Old Testament thing," Acts 9:31 states that the churches in Judea, Galilee, and Samaria *became stronger as the believers lived in the fear of the Lord.*

We are often taught that fear is a bad thing, but fear is not a bad thing at all. In fact, it is a very good thing! Unfortunately, like everything else in our sinful, fallen world, fear can be twisted and corrupted. Yet, at its heart, God created it to be good and to be a blessing.

When a three year-old touches a hot stove, his chubby little fingers get singed and a new fear has entered his young brain. Now, when he sees the stove top glow red, he realizes it is best to stay clear. Fear is keeping him safe.

When a ten year-old me cursed at the babysitter, a new fear entered into me shortly after I heard my father's dress shoes thundering up the steps. I became acutely aware that cursing at the babysitter was most-definitely not a good thing! Fear made me a mannered child!

In truth, there were maybe five or six times in my growing up years that I awaited with dread my father returning home from work. I quickly learned not to do those things again. The fear of punishment kept me from repeating my mistakes and enabled me to be a better person.

Similarly, when we truly understand that God loves us enough to discipline us, a great blessing befalls us. We think twice before doing something that could be potentially dangerous, stupid, sinful, or all three!

In short, the knowledge of consequences makes our choices wiser. Just as fearing there could be a police cruiser around the bend will cause you to stay within the speed limit, so fearing the Lord will cause you to stay within the safe confines of His Word.

Take the issue of pornography for instance (which is discussed at length in a later chapter). The Bible is clear that we should avoid even a hint of sexual immorality.[8] When a healthy fear of the Lord keeps us in obedience to this command, there is blessing. When we discard this command, the results are undeniably tragic.

Studies are now showing that addiction to porn is equal to an addiction to heroin. In fact, the chemicals released in your brain during such viewing actually cause your frontal lobe to shrink. In essence, literally causing brain damage and making it more difficult to form rational decisions.[9]

Research has found that marriages where one person has a porn problem are often plagued by less intimacy and sensitivity, as well as more anxiety, secrecy, isolation, and dysfunction in the relationship. Moreover, since many porn users end up losing their jobs as a result of looking at such things on a company computer, these marriages can end up with less financial security as well. [10]

Divorces related to porn use have "exploded," says Dr. Gary Brooks, a psychologist who has been working with porn addicts for thirty years. Moreover, in a survey of members of the American Academy of Matrimonial Lawyers, sixty-two percent of divorce attorneys surveyed said that obsession with porn had been a significant factor in divorce cases they had handled in the last year. [11]

Indeed, there are consequences for our choices, whether we choose to keep such a thought in our blind spot or not.

A Little Fear Goes a Long Way
I love nature and see it as a great gift from the Lord. I especially love the ocean—its unrivaled vastness and majestic power are amazing. An evening stroll along the surf as the sun sets over an ocean horizon is a little bit of heaven for me.

Yet, while I love the ocean, I also have a healthy fear of it. I am aware that high waves can pound me and push me to the bottom, riptides can pull me from shore and drag me under, jellyfish can sting, crabs can pinch, and then there are the sharks.

I don't know about you, but I am always captivated by Discovery Channel's *Shark Week*. Each year, I am reminded that it would not be a good idea to swim up and pet a great white. Since I like all my limbs right where they are, (and don't ever want to be nicknamed "lefty") I plan on maintaining a safe distance between myself and any dorsal fin I see cutting through the water.

Indeed, I both love and fear the ocean. Likewise, I both love and fear the Lord. His unrivaled vastness and majestic power are beyond compare. His unsurpassed kindness knows no bounds, and His immeasurable grace is fantastically beautiful. Yet, His Holiness burns through whatever I use to cover my sin. His righteousness shines a piercing light into all my dark corners, and His truth cuts like a knife into every lie I tell myself.

Truly, such an understanding of God makes me think twice before sinning. Yet, at the same time, such an understanding also causes me to run to Him when I do sin. I know I may very well experience consequences for my actions, but I further know that His desire is to make me a better person through whatever pain He must put me through.

That, after all, is what good fathers do.

BLIND SPOT
Porn

Allow me a few moments to shock the padoody out of you.

Twelve percent of all websites are pornographic with 266 new porn websites added to the internet every day. There are over 4.2 million of these websites consisting of over 372 million pages. Moreover, there are an estimated 1.5 billion pornographic downloads a month. That number is thirty-five percent of all internet downloads.[1]

Videos watched on Pornhub alone last year exceeded ninety-one *billion*, with over 44,000 visitors per minute![2] On that site, 4.6 *billion* hours of porn were viewed in 2016 alone. It would take over 191 million days (or 5,246 centuries) to reach that many hours, yet that's how much porn was viewed in just one single year![3] And, again, that's just *one* porn site.

Roughly 2.5 billion emails sent or received *every day* contain porn. Every second 28,258 users are watching pornography on the internet. Every second $3,075.64 is being spent on pornography on the internet. Every second 372 people are typing the word "adult" into search engines. Forty million Americans regularly visit porn sites. One quarter of all search engine queries are related to pornography--about sixty-eight million searches a day. Even more disturbing, search engines get 116,000 searches each day related to child pornography, which, by the way, is one of the fastest growing industries in the world with an estimated 624,000 child porn traders in America alone![4]

These are frightening statistics. Statistics that are made even more frightening when you realize that 87% of all twelve to seventeen year-olds in America are using the internet.[5] Speaking of twelve to seventeen year-olds, did you know that their age group is the largest consumer of internet pornography?[6]

Here are a few more did you knows. Did you know that the average age of first exposure to online pornography is age nine? Did you know that 90% of eight to sixteen year-olds have viewed pornography online, most while simply trying to do their homework?[7] Though it's not all by accident. Did you know that "sex" and "porn" were two of the top five words used by *eight to twelve year-olds* on internet search engines?[8]

Do not be fooled. Pornography on the internet is more than abundant, and pornographers are actively working to attract younger and younger viewers. Consider that more than twenty-five children's characters have been found linked to thousands of pornographic websites. Imagine a ten year-old making an online search for a favorite character and being led to places no child, or adult, should ever be.

When I was a teenager, in the mid to late 1980s, pornography was not nearly so easy to find. Usually, it was only available in magazines and videos that were sold in places people under eighteen were not allowed to be. It is not so anymore. Children and teens are just a click or two away from it. To give a child or teen a laptop with no accountability software loaded on, or to set up a computer in their bedroom, is the equivalent of my father handing me a Penthouse magazine when I was a teen and telling me to just read the article about the Porsche.

My father, of course, never did such a thing. He would have known there was no way I was just going to look at pictures of Porches. The temptation to look at other things would have been too great. It is the same with the internet today. We cannot simply set our children and teens up with a computer in their room and say, "Now, this is just for homework and email." The temptation is too great.

When it comes to the internet, I have to wonder: In the history of the world, has there ever been so much good and so much evil in the same place? There is no doubt that internet can be used to do some very positive things. Yet, there is equally no doubt that the internet has a dark underbelly; one that is shockingly easy to find and explore, regardless of your age.

This is Your Brain on Porn
Back in the day, there was a certain commercial that played on TV quite often. In this commercial, a guy held up an egg and said, "This is your brain." Then, he took the egg and cracked it into a skillet. As the egg sizzled in the pan, the man finished with, "This is your brain on drugs." Today, that same commercial could be used for porn.

Researchers have discovered that the brain scans of those high on heroin and the brain scans of those stimulated by porn are nearly identical. In fact, since the brain reacts to visual stimuli quicker than anything else, studies show that the effect of viewing pornography is actually quicker and more severe than taking drugs.

The viewing of pornography releases chemicals in the brain as addicting and as powerful as any drug. These chemicals overrule our rational thought and keep us looking. Gordon Bruin, founder and president of InnerGold Counseling Services, astutely points out the following:

> *Just as Dopamine is the chemical of pleasure, Oxytocin is the chemical of bonding. For example, when a mother gives birth, extreme amounts of Oxytocin are released, creating a powerful emotional bond between mother and child...Oxytocin is also released in high amounts during sexual experiences. This bonding creates companionship and a feeling of togetherness during sexual intercourse.*
>
> *Oxytocin is also released during visual arousal...When sexually aroused without a committed partner through means such as pornography, the recipient of Oxytocin is left feeling alone, depressed and confused, despite the rush of dopamine. See the dangerous irony?*
>
> *Oxytocin has the power to sexually bond a committed couple in healthy and meaningful ways or it can destroy an individual with feelings of emptiness and depression. Oxytocin is a chemical "glue" seeking something to bond with. When there is no bonding, isolation and secrecy result. Pornography is an Oxytocin powerhouse leaving a wake of emptiness and confusion to all those it claims.*[9]

Moreover, studies are now also showing that viewing porn actually damages the part of our brain known as the pre-frontal cortex. This is serious business, especially when you understand that it is the pre-frontal cortex that is the "decision-making" part of the brain. As Luke Gilkerson writes, "When our prefrontal lobes are working properly, we have executive control of the processes going on in our brains. It is where we do our abstract thinking, make goals, solve problems, regulate behavior, and where we suppress emotions, impulses, and urges." However, the flood of chemicals released from our brain's "pleasure center" (known as the limbic system) during the viewing of porn cause all activity in the prefrontal lobes to be overridden.[10]

As with anything, exercise makes things stronger while a lack of exercise makes things weaker. When constantly viewing porn, the pleasure center strengthens rapidly and decisions are no longer made through rational thought but through "feeling." According to the National Center for Biotechnology, feelings of arousal repeatedly winning over rational thought cause the pre-frontal cortex to shrink over time, which further limits the ability to make wise choices in future times of temptation.[11]

Addict See, Addict Do
As we will discuss in the chapter on entertainment choices, there is a direct correlation between what goes into our minds and what comes out through our actions. A very simple Character Formation Formula goes something like this:
- What you put into your heart and mind is what you think about
- What you think about is what you do
- What you do becomes your behavior
- Your behavior becomes your character
- Your character is who you are

With this simple formula, we see that who we are is inextricably determined by the things we choose to mentally chew on, and there is virtually no more poisonous food than porn. Once you start to view pornography, the chemical release in your brain necessitates that you keep viewing. This repeated viewing leads to "do"—usually in the form of chronic masturbation.

However, just as a drug addict needs more and more of a substance to reach the same level of high, so it is with a porn addict. Not reaching the same chemical high, instinctively, the addict will compensate by spending more time and more money viewing porn, often delving into more illicit, violent, and edgy material. (These are often things the addict would have never even considered looking at a few short weeks or months earlier.)[12]

As more violent and coarse material enter the brain, actions begin to change. Masturbation no longer satisfies like before, while aggression towards others increases coupled with improper sexual desires beginning to burgeon. Since porn often shows victims of violent sexual encounters "enjoying" the experience, that only bolsters these violent fantasies. In fact, one study found that those with higher exposure to violent porn were six times more likely to have raped someone than those who had a low exposure.[13]

A person's character totally changes as everything becomes about getting the next fix. Relationships suffer, grades drop, moods swing rapidly, depression and anxiety fill the heart, and more. I could relate story after story from parents, spouses, and children of people they love who've been negatively transformed by the bane of porn.

Instead, I will share with you just these few.

Porn's Effect in Your Home and in the Church

Meet thirteen year-old Timmy. For homework one day, he needed to get information about a prominent building in our nation's capital. He logged onto the computer in his room and typed in the web address his teacher had given. Only, instead of ending it with .gov, he accidentally typed in .com.

Pornographers are well aware of such mistakes, and they do not miss a trick. Timmy ended up on a pornographic website. A wave of excitement and fear crested over him all at once. He actually looked behind him even though he knew he was alone in his room. He must have viewed dozens and dozens of images before a knock on his door told him that dinner was ready. He shut the computer off, but the images remained in his mind. He could not shake them and did not want to.

It didn't take long until every spare moment was spent on that site and others. By the time Timmy was fifteen, he was moody, unable to relate well with parents or peers, a chronic masturbator, and beginning to have dangerous fantasies. One time is truly all it took for his life to be inexorably altered.

Doug lived alone with his mother. His father was long gone and his mother worked long hours to support them both. Most days, Doug would come home from school, do his homework, and then get online to play games and keep himself busy.

One Tuesday afternoon, however, Doug ended up in a chat room. He really connected with another boy his age, named Charlie, who seemed to be living his same lonely life. Charlie was bored too and kept bugging Doug to meet somewhere so they could play. One day, Doug agreed and provided his address. Less than an hour later, "Charlie" showed up. Only Charlie was not twelve. He was forty-nine, and his addiction to porn led him to seek out innocent targets.

The privacy of fourteen year-old Rebecca's bedroom lulled her into a very false sense of security. Using her laptop, she emailed naked pictures of herself to a boyfriend who repeatedly begged her for some. She was not sure why she did it. For giggles, for fun, as a turn on. Whatever her reason, the result changed her forever.

With just one thing on his mind, Rebecca's sixteen year-old boyfriend threatened to show these pictures to his friends at school, and to her parents, if she refused to have intercourse with him. Unable to live with that potential embarrassment, she gave in again and again. A single poor decision had led to a lifetime of regret.

Sadly, Rebecca's situation is becoming all too common among teens, so common that the term "sextortion" was created to describe it. Fellow teens (and adults as well) extort money and sexual favors in return for not exposing compromising pictures. For example, in Yucaipa, California, four ninth graders were charged with distributing child pornography after they received naked pictures of female classmates via their cellphones and uploaded them onto the web. Some might be tempted to think these are isolated incidences. They are not. Police state that this is a growing problem on many middle school and high school campuses.[14] Such is the result when twelve to seventeen year-olds are the largest consumers of online porn.

In the church where I now attend (as a layman not a pastor), I was asked to take a fifteen year-old boy from the church's youth ministry under my wing. He had been found with several pornographic pictures on his phone, along with links to sites, phone numbers for "easy girls," and more. Where did he get all of this? From other boys in the same youth ministry! A large number of them would pass along favorite websites to each other, forward photos they had received, exchanged numbers for girls "to chill with," etc. These are middle suburbia, evangelically churched teens, all addicted to porn and helping each other feed their addiction.

Time for the Church to Step Up
A recent report by the Barna Group found that sixty-four percent of youth pastors, and fifty-seven percent of pastors, struggle with porn addiction.[15] Meanwhile, seven out of ten *lay leaders* view pornography at least once a week, while sixty percent of Christian men and thirty percent of Christian women claim addiction to it.

Of the 10,000 calls, emails, and letters Focus on the Family receives daily, porn represents the number one incoming request for help. *New Man* magazine's most frequent request from readers is to refer them to a service or a ministry that can help them with their sexual temptation.[16] Make no mistake, pornography is without a doubt the biggest problem in your church, yet only seven percent of churches have any program available to deal with it.

Well, it's time for the church to step up.

What you can do in your church: There are some fine resources available. Celebrate Recovery has helped thousands of people, while the Conquer Series has given over 500,000 people in seventy different countries the tools to break free from this scourge. If your church currently has no program in place for people struggling with sex and porn, contact your pastor or leadership team today and let them know about these programs!

What you can do in your home – part 1: Make accountability priority one. Surfing the internet alone in the bedroom, using cellphones without filters where adults are not present isolates our children from the protection of the flock and the Shepherd. In the end, giving our children this privacy doesn't foster responsibility. Instead, it creates a false notion of independence and a dangerous "I'm old enough to handle this" attitude.

The Bible teaches that we need the flock and the Shepherd for protection and accountability. Lone sheep usually end up dead sheep. We, along with our children, need to know that accountability, not privacy, leads to responsibility. Privacy leads to "It's about me" while accountability leads to "It's about what God expects of all those who walk with Him."

What you can do in your home – part 2: God has given us clear boundaries through His Word. Why? So He could imprison us and keep us from enjoying life? Absolutely not! He created these boundaries so we could enjoy the safest and best life possible. Moreover, He has called us to be part of His church, so we could enter into relationships with others who will help us stay in the center of God's will (or His "safety zone" if you will). It is vital that we understand this and then help our children understand this as well.

We must understand that technology is most safely used within God's boundaries. If technology, or anything else, is causing temptation to break free of these boundaries, then it must be removed for the sake of our souls.

It is precisely the boundaries God provides that give us the most freedom and enjoyment with life. Likewise, boundaries with technology, while not perfect, help free us from much of technology's binding and soul-stealing effects. We can more freely enjoy the positive benefits of technology, knowing that with built-in boundaries and accountability we are less likely to succumb to its dark side.

With that in mind, it is vital that we establish clear boundaries for the usage of all technology. Put web browser filters on all computers, laptops, I-pods, smartphones, etc. Keep computers and laptops in a central area with the screens facing outward. Have a storage area for all portable electronic devices in your room. That is where they all should be stored before bed.

This is not just for kids and teens by the way. For myself, I have accountability and filtering software on both my phone and laptop. My accountability partner gets an email from this software once a week which details all the sites I visited on my computer. Meanwhile, I allowed him to set the parental controls on my phone and only he knows the passcode.

Stay Alert
Sometimes I go to the zoo and I hear people say, "Why is that monkey's butt blue!?!" That question, though, doesn't have anything to do with how I am wrapping things up, so we won't dwell on it.

The other thing that I often hear at the zoo is this, "Animals shouldn't be caged up. They should be free to roam in their natural habitat." When I hear that I both agree and disagree. Surely, God did not intend for His creation to be caged up, but equally as sure, no animal truly roams freely.

Lions in the wild may have more space to roam. Yet when they roam into another pride's territory, they will be attacked without mercy. Similarly, a meerkat family may have more room to roam in the wild. Yet when that family roams into another meerkat family's territory, they also will be viciously attacked.

The point, you ask? None of us are ever truly free. There is always danger, which makes the need for boundaries and accountability incredibly important. Don't ever think, "Not me." "Not my husband." "Not my kids." In 1 Thessalonians 5:6, Paul writes, *so be on your guard, not asleep like the others. Stay alert and be clearheaded.* Peter reaffirms this in 1 Peter 5:8, *stay alert! Watch out for your great enemy, the devil. He prowls around like a roaring lion, looking for someone to devour.*

We would all be wise to heed those words. The need to stay alert to protect our families is greater than ever.

Note to parents: Be aware that blocking the internet, especially on phones, may not be sufficient. Social media apps like Instagram, Twitter, Tumblr, Snapchat, and more have an abundance of porn. (In fact, SnapChat was created to make sharing porn easier and more discreet.) Moreover, some apps, like the music app Shazam and the Facebook app, allow users to bypass parental controls and access the internet.

BLIND SPOT
Entertainment Standards

One day a beleaguered father listened to all the reasons his children gave for wanting to see a particular PG-13 movie. It had their favorite actors. Everyone else was seeing it. Even church members said it was great. It was only rated PG-13 because of the suggestion of sex--they never really showed any of it.

The language was pretty good too--the Lord's name was only used in vain three whole times in the entire movie, and there were just like a dozen or so uses of foul language. The teens did admit to a scene where a bunch of people were blown up, but the violence was just the normal stuff. It wasn't too bad. And, even if there were a few minor things, the special effects were fabulous and the plot was action packed.

However, even with all the justifications the teens made for the movie's rating, the father still wouldn't give in. Finally tired of constantly discussing it, he thought up an original idea. A little later that evening, Dad asked his sons if they would like some brownies he had baked. He explained that he'd taken the family's favorite recipe and added a little something new. The boys asked what it was.

The father calmly replied that he had added dog poop. However, he quickly assured them, it was only a little bit. All other ingredients were gourmet quality, and he had taken great care to bake the brownies at the precise temperature for the exact time. He was sure the brownies would be superb.

Even with their father's promise that the brownies were of almost perfect quality, the teens would not dig in. Dad acted quite surprised. After all, it was only one small part that was causing them to be so stubborn. He assured them again that they would hardly notice. Still, the boys held firm and would not try the brownies.

The father then explained how the movie they wanted to see was just like the brownies. The devil works to make us believe that just a little bit of evil won't matter. But, the truth is even a little bit of poop makes the difference between a great treat and something totally unacceptable. Dad went on to explain that even though the entertainment industry would have us believe that most of today's movies, television shows, video games, and music are acceptable for adults and youth, often they are not.

Today, when this creative dad's kids want to see something that contains questionable material, he merely asks them if they would like some of his special brownies.[1]

Making the Heart and Mind a "No Poo Zone"
Most of us (I hope) wouldn't eat a brownie with poo in it. No matter how small the amount, we simply don't want excrement in our stomachs. Yet, how many of us don't seem to care about the poo that sits in our hearts and minds through movies, music, TV, internet, video games, and more? Strange, isn't it? Why do we think it is better to have poo in our hearts and minds than in our stomachs?

Look at what the Bible says about this. Jesus tells His disciples in Mark 7:19-22, *"Food doesn't go into your heart, but only passes through the stomach and then goes into the sewer." (By saying this, he declared that every kind of food is acceptable in God's eyes.) And then he added, "It is what comes from inside that defiles you. For from within, out of a person's heart, come evil thoughts, sexual immorality, theft, murder, adultery, greed, wickedness, deceit, lustful desires, envy, slander, pride, and foolishness."*

The Lord seems clear that our hearts and minds are significantly more important than our stomachs. The reason? Food will not ruin our lives, but our thoughts will. This is why the Bible further states, *Guard your heart above all else, for it determines the course of your life.*[2]

God's Word discusses *a lot* of important things. So, if there is a part that announces, "Above all of those important things, focus on guarding your heart," then we should see that as a very big deal. Why? Well, look what else Jesus says. *"A good person produces good things from the treasury of a good heart, and an evil person produces evil things from the treasury of an evil heart. What you say flows from what is in your heart."*[3]

Whatever is in your heart will determine what you say and how you act. This is why Solomon would write in Proverbs, *as a face is reflected in water, so the heart reflects the real person.*[4] In other words, our hearts reflects the real us. Whatever we allow into our hearts will determine who and what we will be like.

Consider the Character Formation Formula we looked at earlier in the book.

- What you put into your heart and mind is what you think about

- What you think about is what you do
- What you do becomes your behavior
- Your behavior becomes your character
- Your character is who you are

Looking at this formula again, we see that who we are and who we will become is determined all the way back at the beginning of the formula by what we allow into our hearts and minds. This is why the Bible instructs us to, *above all else*, guard what we allow into our hearts and minds. What we do, what we say, and who we really are is determined by what's in our hearts.

If we stuff our hearts and minds with movies, music, video games, and websites filled with sexuality, violence, foul language, blasphemy, unbiblical themes, and more, these things will create thoughts. Those thoughts will lead to actions. Those actions will lead to a pattern of behavior. That pattern of behavior will become our character, and who we are has been established.

Eye Openers
Certainly, this is a major blind spot in our culture today, even among Christians. Many of us make plans to watch TV shows and movies without thinking for a moment about the content. How many times on social media have you read about a fellow Christian's excitement over seeing a certain movie set to come out, even though he or she has no idea what content issues it may contain? Just recently, a Christian friend of mine, snowed in and missing work, excitedly announced on Facebook that she was going to spend the "snowpocalypse" bingeing Game of Thrones. What the what!

Consider the extent of this blind spot with the following analogy. Imagine that after a long and exhausting day, you climb into a warm and relaxing shower. You want to wash the day away and allow your muscles to calm as the steamy water pulsates over your skin. You're lost in the bliss of it all when suddenly you hear rustling outside your bathroom window.

Glancing over, you notice a dark figure peering in the window. Instantly, you start screaming and shouting, startling the voyeur, who immediately flees into the blackness of the night. Without fully drying off, you call the police and frantically inform them of the "pervert" who was trying to eye you up.

Certainly, you would be justified to label that individual a "pervert." In fact, should he be caught, he would be labeled a sex offender and rightly so. Without a doubt, peeking through someone's window screen hoping to see nakedness or sexuality is perverted and wrong.

Yet, let's change the phrase "window screen" to TV screen, movie screen, or computer screen. Suddenly, viewing the same types of things is no longer considered perverted or wrong in our culture. If I were to burst into your living room while you were watching something sensual on TV and labeled you a pervert, you would instantly argue back, "Hey, I'm no pervert." But do you keep watching TV shows, going to movies, surfing websites, and playing video games with sexual material?

If you've never considered that seeking nudity through a window screen is no different than seeking it through a TV or computer screen, then that should be a good indicator of how our culture has corrupted the way you think. Our culture has conditioned us to believe it's no big deal. In fact, Hollywood regularly fills shows and movies with sex, and video game creators, webmasters, and songwriters do the same, in the hopes that it will encourage us to watch or play or listen.

All the while God's Word says things like, ***have nothing*** *to do with sexual immorality, impurity, lust, and evil desires* (emphasis mine).[5]

*Let there be **no sexual immorality**, impurity, or greed among you. Such sins have no place among God's people* (emphasis mine).[6]

Run from sexual sin![7]

You can take it to the bank that if what is in your heart determines the course of your life, then Satan is going to try to get whatever he can in there. Of course, he knows he would never attract us with things that are dull and boring. No, instead, he makes it all seem good by surrounding it with big budget Hollywood special effects, a funny script, great graphics, a catchy tune, etc. It's really no different than when Eve took the apple because the devil made it look so *pleasing to the eye.*[8]

The movies nominated for the Best Picture Oscar in 2014 totaled forty-four sex scenes, 176 times instances of blasphemy, and 1212 curse words. None of those totals, by the way, include the unbiblical themes that were pervasive throughout. If you averaged out these things between the nominated movies that makes an average of five sex scenes, twenty instances of blasphemy, and 135 curse words per movie. Which means, for a two hour movie, you would get a sex scene every twenty-four minutes, the Lord's name abused every six minutes, and a curse word every fifty-three seconds! Call me crazy, but I doubt God cast His vote for any of those nominated movies.

Please understand, this is a *huge* blind spot in our culture-- movies, TV shows, music, video games, books, magazines, and more are filled with content that clutters our heart, deadens the fire of the faith, and distracts us from our mission. Just because the culture says it's "Oscar worthy" that doesn't mean God does. Instead of being a blockbuster, it could very well be a soul buster.

Just recently, I was talking about this very subject with someone. The person, who is Christian, said to me. "Well, you know, I watch all of this stuff, but I don't even notice content issues anymore, or I just choose to ignore them and focus on the story." This person is not alone.

But what must God think about what we are becoming as a society? How does He feel as Christians flow along with the culture's standards for movies, music, video games, thought-life, web surfing, respect toward authority, attitudes with others, stances on contemporary issues, etc.? When sin becomes so common that we don't notice it anymore, then that's a blind spot too big to ignore any longer.

Real Life vs. the Shadowlands
God's plan is for our behavior and our choices to show that He is first in our lives. God's plan is for us and our families to avoid things that lead to impurity, lust, vulgarity, coarseness, and greed. Unfortunately, most of us make decisions based on what we want not on what God wants. Because of this, we regularly indulge in the things the Lord would have us avoid. When questioned about these choices, the most common reply is, "Well, after all, it's just showing 'real life.'"

Please understand that what Hollywood offers is *nothing* close to real life. Real life is found in Christ. This world, as CS Lewis famously pointed out, is just the Shadowlands. The Bible says that real life is found in the Lord and that, as Christians, we are citizens of heaven. *Since you have been raised to new life with Christ, set your sights on the realities*

61

*of heaven, where Christ sits in the place of honor at God's right hand. Think about the things of heaven, not the things of earth. For you died to this life, and **your real life is hidden with Christ in God**. And when Christ, who is your life, is revealed to the whole world, you will share in all his glory* (emphasis mine).[9]

Hollywood doesn't know a thing about real life. What Hollywood offers is the Shadowlands. So if you want the Shadowlands, then Hollywood is your answer. However, if you yearn for real life, then you need to embrace Christ. For it is only in Christ that you can find real life.

When a shepherd is training sheep to follow him, he does not take them to a lion and say "Now, this a lion." He does not take them to a wolf and say "Now, this a wolf." Instead, a shepherd will speak to the sheep over and over, so that his voice is imprinted on their minds. When that happens, thirty people can call for that sheep, but it will only go to its shepherd.

That's what I want for my family and for yours. I want us to know Christ and real life so well that when the counterfeits start calling to us, we run to our Shepherd. In my home, we hardly watch any movies at all. We barely watch any program television, and we generally only listen to Christian radio. Because of these choices, I have been called a Pharisee, legalist, and even a Christian Nazi. (I am not exactly sure what that is, but I am pretty sure it isn't a good thing!).

Nevertheless, I want my family to focus on the real thing. I want to center on the things of God. I want to imitate God. I want to follow Christ. I want to love sin less every day and love God more every day. I want my son to grow up knowing the real thing, the only thing that truly matters. I want those around me to see me going after the real thing, not the sin-warped shadowlands. Yes, I want these things. I need these things.

Do I succeed all the time? NO! I have a line of friends and family who can share with you all my many failures (and probably do it eagerly), but God's best is what I want. And listen, if those around you know that is what you want, even when you fail only to get back up again, that may encourage them to rise in the midst of their failures as well.

The "reality" of Hollywood is its product lessens God's precious name in our hearts and minds by its repeated vain and improper use of it. It fills our hearts and minds with foul language and sexual promiscuity. It teaches us to handle issues in our own wisdom instead of God's wisdom. It normalizes what the Bible calls sin and lures us into its pleasures, causing us to ignore or excuse the "poo" to keep enjoying it.

To know Christ and become like Him is the goal of life. The goal is not to know the world and become like it, not to be able to list all the latest contemporary singers, not to have seen all the latest movies, and not to know what happened in the latest episode of *This is Us*.

I have had the privilege of seeing many people come to Christ, and none of them did so because I knew about the latest movie. It was because they saw me pursuing the real thing, even in failure, and they wanted it too.

Living by the Code
In the 1930s, Hollywood developed "The Hays Code." This code created censorship guidelines which dictated what actors could or could not say and do or not do on camera. In 1968, Hollywood did away with this code and went to a voluntary ratings system. Without that code, Hollywood, and our culture,

have steadily lowered their standards for sexuality, indecency, foul language, violence, and more.

Regardless of what Hollywood and our culture do, however: we Christians still have a code. It is called the Bible! Today, however, many Christians can be found saying things like, "Yeah, I watch certain TV shows and movies that I probably shouldn't, but it's not like I've seen *Deadpool*." Suddenly, a raunchy movie is the standard we use to judge acceptability, not God's Word.

Some will say, "Yes, I play rated-M video games, but it's not like I'm playing *Grand Theft Auto V*. That's really bad." Again, a crude game becomes the standard with which we judge our choices, not God's Word.

In everyday life we also experience this. "I probably use too much profanity, but I am nothing like Jack. That guy curses like a drunken sailor." Well, is Jack your standard for speech or is God's Word? All the while, each time we reject God's standards for doing whatever *[we] feel like whenever [we] feel like it, and grabbing whatever attracts [our] fancy*, our Heavenly Father is grieved.

Instead of thinking about sin as Christ does, we are actually entertained by it. Instead of putting sin to death, we can't wait for the next episode. Instead of turning our backs on a thought, we choose to dwell on it because we think it gives us pleasure. All the while, as we discussed in the chapter on sin, God passionately and totally hates it. His heart grieves because, instead of pursuing holiness and seeking after what is true, right, noble, pure, lovely, excellent, admirable, and worthy of praise,[10] we pursue what the culture pursues, which is often wrong, ignoble, dirty, distasteful, shameful, and worthy of nothing.

I think it's time I started making some changes to what I consider entertainment. What about you? If so, consider the Bible's "code" for the following:

Sexuality: Earlier in this chapter, we looked at Scripture that challenged us to avoid all sexual sin, to the point of running from it! Jesus takes this one step further by stating, *"So if your eye—even your good eye—causes you to lust, gouge it out and throw it away. It is better for you to lose one part of your body than for your whole body to be thrown into hell."*[11] When the Lord says, "Hey, it's better for you to lose body parts than to be tempted to lust by looking at certain things," that's a pretty good reason to be more discerning with our entertainment choices!

As we discussed in the chapter on porn, sexuality captivates the human brain, causing the release of chemicals that drive us to want more. This is why the Bible calls for "fleeing" such sin and why Jesus uses such strong language in the above Scripture. Sexuality was created by God for a man and woman to enjoy within the confines of marriage. It was never meant to be entertainment for the general public.

In regards to purity, we are instructed to keep ourselves pure just as Christ is pure.[12] And not only keep ourselves pure but to be an example in purity to others.[13] With this in mind, we should ask ourselves if our choices for movies, TV shows, music, video games, internet sites, books, and more are the choices Christ would make. If not, perhaps we are not quite being the examples we should.

Foul Language: In Colossians we read, *but now is the time to* ***cast off*** *and* ***throw away*** *all these rotten garments of anger, hatred, cursing, and dirty language.*[14] Ephesians 5 builds on this by stating, *dirty stories, foul talk, and coarse jokes—**these are not for you**. Instead, remind each other of God's* *goodness, and be thankful* (emphasis mine).[15] We also read, *don't use foul or abusive language. Let everything you say be good and helpful, so that your words will be an encouragement to those who hear them.*[16]

A study done by the Parents Television Council found that profanity on broadcast television networks increased over 70% in just a five year period. Meanwhile, CBS News published results of a Brigham Young study which found "Children exposed to profanity in the media think that such language is 'normal,' which may reduce their inhibitions about using profanity themselves." The study further discovered that children and teens who engage in entertainment filled with profanity tend to be more aggressive and thus more likely to hit, kick, and punch others, or engage in non-physical aggressive behavior like gossiping and spreading rumors about someone.[17]

There are many recent studies available showing the negative effects of profanity in entertainment. (Feel free to do your own research.) These negatives, by the way, do not just effect children and teens but adults as well. The more it is heard in entertainment, the more it is normalized, making it an ever growing part of society. With all that is at stake, I wonder, do we want to be part of the problem or part of the solution?

Blasphemy: The Lord instructs us in the Ten Commandments not to take His name in vain.[18] The word the Lord chooses for "vain" in that passage is a Hebrew word that means "emptiness," "nothingness" or "worthlessness." This, of course, is the exact opposite of what we should be doing with God's name. We are called to bring glory to God and magnify His name.

The Bible repeatedly uses phrases like "Glory of God," "God of glory," "King of glory," and "the glory of the Lord." Many times, the word used for "glory" in the Bible actually has the exact opposite meaning of "vain." It carries with it the idea of substance and weight and dignity. So to use the Lord's name in vain is to do the direct opposite of what God has told us to do with His infinitely precious name.

Meanwhile, the Psalms also tell us things like, *O magnify the Lord with me, and let us exalt His name together.*[19] As well as, *I will praise the name of God with song and magnify Him with thanksgiving.*[20]

Of course, to magnify something is to make it bigger and greater. With that in mind, we should ask ourselves, what happens when the media we and our children ingest constantly bombard us with the vain use of God's name? What happens when we and our children hear His name used again and again as nothing more than a curse word or something to say when you are shocked or excited?

Consider that each vain use, each use that treats God's name as worthless or nothing, eats away at the glory and majesty of His name in our souls. Slowly, over time, God's name simply becomes common and not worth much more than the breath it takes to pass it over our lips whenever we are shocked or excited. It is no longer glorious, weighty, infinitely precious and worthy of our greatest magnification. I don't want to go there. Do you?

Violence: University of Michigan professor L. Rowell Huesmann argues that fifty years of evidence show that exposure to media violence causes children to behave more aggressively and affects them years later as adults.[21] The fifty years that Professor Huesmann refers to dates to research that began in the 1960s regarding violence in the media. Over one thousand studies (including a Surgeon General's special report and a National Institute of Mental Health report) attest to at least some connection between media violence and aggressive behavior in children.[22]

According to the American Psychiatric Association, "The debate is over… For the last three decades, the one predominant finding in research on the mass media is that exposure to media portrayals of violence increases aggressive behavior in children."[23] (9)

Isaiah 26:3 boldly proclaims, *[God], you will keep in perfect peace all who trust in you, whose thoughts are fixed on you!* Peace within the soul comes as we turn our eyes off of worldly entertainment and onto the Lord. Sadly, with our families spending so many hours with entertainment media each week (see below), and so little time in church or devotions, our souls are filled with violent images and not the peace that God, through Christ, so desires to bring. Violence in the media indeed acts like spiritual plaque which narrows the entryway to the soul choking out the flow of peace our Creator wishes to pour into us.

Time: In the Psalms, Moses asks the Lord to *teach us to realize the brevity of life…*[24] King David echoed those sentiments when he wrote, *You have made my life no longer than the width of my hand. My entire lifetime is just a moment to you; at best, each of us is but a breath.*"[25] And in the New Testament, James reminds that *your life is like the morning fog—it's here a little while, then it's gone.*[26]

Each of us has only so many days on this earth to make an impact for eternity. How wisely are we using our time? Statistics show not too well. A recent study by the Nielson Company stated that the average American spent ten hours and thirty-nine minutes a day in "screen time" in 2016.[27] Not to be outdone, statista.com showed the average American is spending 721 minutes a day with media of our culture.[28] That's over twelve hours a day!

Compare that to the amount of time spent in church, in prayer, and in devotions each day. For most of us, the two don't compare well! We spend way too much time with the culture and not nearly enough with Christ. Consider also that 1 Corinthians 15:33 states that *bad company corrupts good character.* Company, of course, is *not* just people. It is anyone or anything we spend time with. So what kind of company are we keeping, and how much is that "company" rubbing off on us?

Frankly, even if we remove unbiblical content issues from the equation, it is overly evident that we are captivated by our culture and what it has to offer. Spending up to half the day with movies, TV shows, the internet, video games, etc. will most definitely lessen the fire of our faith, distract us from our purpose, keep us from investing in relationships, and also from sharing our faith.

How about you and your family? How well are you redeeming the time? Many Christians lament the state of the entertainment industry, yet continue to ingest it all. Please understand that the entertainment industry doesn't care about our complaints, only our money and time. If we continue to buy the tickets, download the albums, turn on the shows, and play the video games, we're saying with our money and time, "Yes, more of this, please."

Mark Your Home a Safe Harbor
"Should we shut ourselves off from the world then?" Some people ask. "After all, there is cursing and blasphemy and foul language and underdressed people out there." I understand why some people would say such things. But the fact is that going out into the world to reflect Christ to those who

desperately need Him is not optional. Meanwhile, our entertainment choices are.

We cannot effectively do the non-negotiable part, reflecting Christ, if we continually allow His image in us to be effected by all the "poo" of the world. To best reflect Christ we must fight to make sure our homes are governed by choices and standards that please Him. Our homes should be refuges from the storms of life and safe havens from the effects of the culture. Our homes should be places that even visitors recognize as special and divinely blessed. In other words, our homes should be marked as God's territory.

Our children, friends, neighbors, classmates, and coworkers need to see that God owns our home. God owns the TV; God owns the radio; God owns the computers; God owns the video game system; God owns the magazines; God owns the magnets on the refrigerator; God owns the pictures on the wall; God owns the posters in the bedroom, and God owns the words we say and the actions we use. Home is to be a place where we can experience and practice how God would have us live out our lives in the world.

Unfortunately, often times what happens is the opposite. As we walk in the world, the culture infects our souls. When we enter our homes, the infection spreads. Soon our homes are not governed by the expectations of God, rather they are governed by what the culture thinks is cool. Choices then are not made with biblical standards. They are made by other factors such as: What the kids at school are doing, what everyone is talking about at work, what movie promises to be a blockbuster, what the latest "must see TV" is, or what the newest commercial says I should buy or do.

The church I pastored while living in rural Wisconsin was about a half mile from a pig enclosure that housed roughly five thousand of our pink-skinned pals. If you've never had the displeasure of being near such an enclosure, I can tell you that it takes stink to a whole new level! When the wind blew just right, that reek travelled to the church and hung over it like a pall. The stench stuck to your clothes like some sort of evil glue and literally made breathing difficult! Coming home from working at the church, I would actually have to take my clothes off in the garage in order to not bring that awful stink into my house. (And people wonder why I don't like bacon!)

The negative effects of the culture act the same way, and we must fight against bringing those effects into our homes. Our homes should be governed by God. Everyone who enters should feel as though they have entered a refuge and a place of rest from the storm. It should be a place of safety for the body and the mind. It should be a place where the soul can be filled with the greatness of God.

BLIND SPOT
The Need for Transformation

In my book, *Living Above the Line: Pursuing Christ-likeness in a Post-Christian culture,* I speak about how Adam's fall seems to have rewired our DNA. Instead of running away from the sin, we run towards it. Instead of denying its temptations, we desire them. We see this clearly in CS Lewis' amazing work *The Screwtape Letters*. In this excellent book, a senior demon, Screwtape, is seeking to disciple his young nephew. In one particular letter, Screwtape is comforting his nephew who is despairing because his "patient" just accepted the Lord.

Screwtape writes, "There is no need to despair; hundreds of these adult converts have been reclaimed after a brief sojourn in the Enemy's camp and are now with us. *All the habits of the patient, both mental and bodily, are still in our favor*" (emphasis mine).

Isn't that the truth?

I remember a time when my nephew, only eleven months at the time, stood on wobbly legs using a coffee table to support his uneasy gait. In the center of that table was an "untouchable." But, oh, how young Andrew wanted to touch it. Reaching out his pudgy little arm, he strained to get his stubby fingers on it.

"Noooo! Don't touch." The stern voice of my brother-in-law got Andrew's attention. He quickly recoiled his arm.

A few seconds later, Andrew turned his bald head my brother-in-law's way. When he didn't see Daddy watching, he reached again. Slowly, his arm stretched toward the forbidden…then pause, followed by a furtive glance Dad's way once again.

It was almost comical as I watched it unfold. I could practically see the gears spinning in his year-old brain as he tried to figure out how to touch the centerpiece without my brother-in-law seeing. Still unable to form full sentences, he could still form self-centered thoughts and desires for what he was not allowed to have.

Rewind a few years, and I have my own two year-old zipping around the house with a toy truck. He is given free reign with that truck, so long as he does not bang it into the wall. What does he do? He takes that truck right up to the edge. The bumper almost kisses the molding as he looks back at me. Catching my gaze, he zooms the truck away only to come back a few moments later.

Again, with microscopic distance between the truck bumper and the pristine white molding, he searches for me from the corners of his eyes. My voice gets his full attention. "Touch the wall with that truck, and I'll take the truck. And, boy, you'll be in trouble!"

Time for a New Identity

Are my nephew and son the only ones who do such things? Not even close. We are all like this. Screwtape's point is one we should carefully consider--our thoughts, desires, and habits seem bent toward sin. The Bible makes this same point when it states, *all have sinned and fallen short of the glory of God.*[1]

In other words, sin has genetically disposed us to be line breakers. Our rebel hearts find that living above the line is hard and boring. Meanwhile, living across the line seems easy and exciting. True, we know we shouldn't live too far over the line. But if we're close enough to give it a hug once and awhile, then that's not so bad. It's as though we think being a Christian is just about being closer to "the good side" of the line than those who are not Christian.

The Bible, however, says it's time to adjust our side views and get that thought out of the blind spot. *[Jesus] died for everyone so that those who receive his new life will no longer live to please themselves. Instead, they will live to please Christ, who died and was raised for them... What this means is that **those who become Christians become new persons. They are not the same anymore, for the old life is gone. A new life has begun**! (Emphasis mine.)*[2]

Being a Christian is much more than not being a sinner. Christianity is about grabbing hold of a new identity. We were once people outside of a relationship with the God of the universe, but now we are in a relationship with Him. Such a radical relationship change requires a radical lifestyle change.

Another way to look at this is to consider a wedding ceremony. Imagine you are sitting in a sanctuary on a beautiful Saturday morning. The procession of the bridal party has just ended. A silence falls over the church. Instinctively, you turn your head toward the back of that sun-drenched sanctuary. You know the bride is near.

Then you hear it. The dulcet tones of "Here Comes the Bride" reverberate through the brass pipes of an old church organ. All eyes catch hold of a woman in white. As this dazzling woman walks down the aisle, you get a firsthand look at someone in transition. This young lady is moving from single to married. She is moments away from being called "wife," signifying a new and intimate relationship with another.

This soon-to-be bride is going from "Status: single" to "Status: married." And because this is so, that means things will change. Always going out with her girlfriends, dating other guys, leaning on her parents for advice; all of that will now change. Not because there are "new rules" that she need be legalistic over, but because she is in a new kind of relationship.

It is this very idea that Paul keys on in Colossians 3:7-11. *You used to do [sinful deeds] when your life was still part of this world. But now is the time to get rid of anger, rage, malicious behavior, slander, and dirty language. Don't lie to each other, for you have stripped off your old evil nature and all its wicked deeds. In its place you have clothed yourselves with a brand-new nature that is continually being renewed as you learn more and more about Christ, who created this new nature within you. In this new life, it doesn't matter if you are a Jew or a Gentile, circumcised or uncircumcised, barbaric, uncivilized, slave, or free. Christ is all that matters, and he lives in all of us.*

Perhaps, before marriage, our new bride went out three to four evenings a week with her girlfriends. Perhaps she used to date other guys regularly. Perhaps she leaned on her father for all problems and issues that emerged. But now she is married. Now she is something new—a wife.

Her primary relationship is with her husband now. She should spend her evenings with him, not continuing to date other guys or constantly hanging with her girlfriends. She should seek his advice when problems arise, not her father's. Everything has changed. Not because there are new rules but because there is a new relationship.

It is the same, Paul tells us in Colossians, for those of us who have accepted Christ. We used to do *whatever [we] feel like whenever [we] feel like it, and grabbing whatever attracts [our] fancy.* We stepped over the line for all sorts of reasons, but we are in a new relationship now. Things need to change.

Multiple times in Scripture, God's people are referred to as "the bride."[3] That means we don't flirt with the world any longer, and we don't act single. It's time to send divorce papers to the world's lawyers because Christ is our focus now. He is all that matters.

A New Reality

If you are in a relationship with the Creator of the universe, then you must make new lines to guard that relationship. Just as a single woman becoming a bride should change her lifestyle, so our relationship with the Lord should change our lives. In fact, it should change every aspect of our lives.

Paul also discusses this in Colossians 3. *Since you have been raised to new life with Christ, set your sights on the realities of heaven, where Christ sits at God's right hand in the place of honor and power. Let heaven fill your thoughts. Do not think only about things down here on earth. For you died when Christ died, and your real life is hidden with Christ in God. And when Christ, who is your real life, is revealed to the whole world, you will share in all his glory. So put to death the sinful, earthly things lurking within you. Have nothing to do with sexual sin, impurity, lust, and shameful desires. Don't be greedy for the good things of this life, for that is idolatry.*[4]

Just as getting married should cause a fundamental shift in

your view of reality, so Paul says that our new relationship with God should do the same. It is no longer, "Hey, I'm single and I can do what I want, whenever I want."

When you get married, all of that changes. You don't go where you want whenever you want. You don't do what you want whenever you want, and you don't buy what you want whenever you want. Why not? Because you have someone else to consider. You have someone else's wishes, dreams, goals, and ideas to take into account and to care about.

Before I was married, I made major purchases by myself, planned vacations by myself, created schedules for myself, and, hey, I even dressed myself. Today, I wouldn't dare make a major purchase by myself. (I can't anyway. My wife carries the checkbook.) I don't make plans without considering my wife (because I like to sleep in a bed and not on the sofa), and I have to go through the fashion police before I head out the door.

As Christians, it is the same thing. There has to be a fundamental shift in how we think about reality. If I am in a relationship with the Creator, and He has a will and a plan and purpose for my life, I need to make those things paramount.

Our new life in Christ requires a new focus--a focus on Him, on the things that please Him, and on the things that will help us live our lives as examples for a watching world. But you remember our problem, right? While God hates sin, we desire it. All our thoughts and habits are bent toward giving ourselves pleasure. So we put the need for transformation in our blind spot and continue driving without considering if perhaps we should be in the passenger seat and God should be the one behind the wheel.

Turning in Your Cracked Bucket

If you turned to Jeremiah 2 in your Bible, you would know that it was not going to be a pleasant read just by the chapter heading! Depending on your translation, you might read titles like, "The Results of Israel's Sin," "Israel Forsakes God," and "Judah's Apostasy." Not good!

Once in the chapter itself, you quickly find that the Lord is quite perturbed with the Israelites for their repeated disobedience. After listing off the many ways He has cared for them and watched over them, God laments:

"For my people have done two evil things: They have forsaken me -- the fountain of living water. And they have dug for themselves cracked cisterns that can hold no water at all!"[5]

Keeping with this theme, a few verses later God questions, *"What have you gained by your alliances with Egypt and Assyria? What good to you are the waters of the Nile and the Euphrates?"*[6]

To fully appreciate what the Lord is saying here, we have to understand a few things. In our day and age, with water taps in all our kitchens and bathrooms, we struggle to appreciate just how vital water is to our survival. In Bible times, however, rivers were life. All major cities and towns were near rivers. All agriculture occurred near rivers. The heart of any ancient civilization beat by a river.

The Nile and the Euphrates were especially important because both were in arid environments. The Egyptians and Assyrians relied on these respective rivers for water, for fishing, for irrigation, for everything. These rivers meant survival.

So when God asks, "What have you gained by your alliances with Egypt and Assyria? What good to you are the waters of the Nile and the Euphrates?" He is really saying, "You have crossed the line in an effort to find life apart from Me. You are seeking to center on things other than Me, and what has it gotten you?"

The Lord lets them know that He alone is the fountain of life. There is hope, fulfillment, joy, and peace only in Him. Yet, the Israelites have taken their cracked buckets to lesser streams. Trying to fill themselves with all that the world offered, they stubbornly refused to admit that their buckets were empty. The few drops clinging to the bottom of the bucket were their only reward for rejecting the fountain of life.

In our culture, life is not centered on rivers. Rather it is centered on self. That is, on the selfish pursuit of our own pleasure and dream fulfillment. We leave the fountain of life because the rivers of Hollywood promise us pleasure and happiness. We forsake the fountain of life because streaming from the internet is one dalliance after another that we hope will satiate us. We turn our back on the fountain of life because God's plans seem dull and boring and the world seems to offer so much.

We flee the fountain of life for the drying creek beds of sex, porn, money, fame, possessions, and career. Yet, in spite of all our effort, the cracked buckets we carry cannot satisfy our thirst. Instead of separating from the world, we drift from God and the results are never good. Sin never delivers. Crossing over to dip our buckets in forbidden rivers leaves us feeling dry and empty.

In Christ Alone
People spend their days seeking fulfillment and satisfaction in just about everything but Jesus. And, not so surprisingly, never really seem to find it. There's a reason why Americans take

more antidepressant drugs than any other country. Get this. It is estimated that one out of every six Americans is on some sort of psychiatric medication.

Here we are, one of the richest countries in the history of the world, with all the latest and coolest gadgets, the most-expensive movie budgets, the largest amount of video games, more TV channels than you can imagine, parks, pools, golf courses, malls, etc. So much! Yet, we lead the world in the use of antidepressants.

Non-Christians buy the lie that they don't need Jesus, while Christians buy the lie that they can just add Jesus to their lives, get an insurance policy for Heaven, and nothing needs to change. Meanwhile, the devil seeks to distract us with movies, music, games, the internet, sports, and more. Now, we are too busy going from one fleeting thrill to another to realize what's just out of view.

Seventeenth century philosopher and scientist, Blaise Pascal, stated, "There is a God-shaped vacuum in the heart of every man which cannot be filled by any created thing, but only by God, the Creator, made known through Jesus." In other words, he's saying, "There is a God-sized hole in each man's heart."

Obviously, you can stuff millions of dollars, tons of possessions, boyfriend after boyfriend, girlfriend after girlfriend, etc. into that hole, but you cannot fill it. Only God can fill a God-sized hole. And He does not fill that hole because you prayed a prayer once and asked Jesus into your heart. No, He fills your heart and life as you seek to become more and more like Christ with each and every passing day.

Time to be Diligent
Just the day before I sat to write this chapter, I heard a pastor

say these words, "God's grace is opposed to earning, but it is not opposed to effort. God expects you to work hard, to be diligent, and to protect your heart and mind."

Many people grab hold of God's great grace, through the cross of Christ, and then believe that His grace covers them so they can live as they please. Yet, God's grace was never meant to create excuses for our behavior or to reduce our effort.

It was meant to show us that we are helplessly lost without His intervention, for there is no way that we can earn our salvation. The gift of faith in Christ's death and resurrection is the only path to Heaven. As it tells us in Ephesians 2:8, *for it is by grace you have been saved, through faith--and this not from yourselves, it is the gift of God.*

Yet, this gift of grace can never be an excuse to sin or to reduce our effort. Romans 6 makes this abundantly clear. *What should we say then? Should we keep on sinning so that God's grace can increase? Not at all! As far as sin is concerned, we are dead. So how can we keep on sinning? All of us were baptized into Christ Jesus. Don't you know that we were baptized into his death? By being baptized, we were buried with Christ into his death. Christ has been raised from the dead by the Father's glory. And like Christ we also can live a new life...So don't let sin rule your body, which is going to die. Don't obey its evil longings. Don't give the parts of your body to serve sin. Don't let them be used to do evil. Instead, give yourselves to God. You have been brought from death to life. Give the parts of your body to him to do what is right.[7]*

So be diligent my friends. Work hard. Set aside time to pray and to seek God's strength, to read the Bible, and to tap into God's wisdom. Be sure to surround yourself with accountability partners who will help you pursue Christ-likeness.

Fight against your natural sinfulness, yearn to be free from old habits, and understand there is only emptiness apart from the fountain of life. Christ-likeness is our goal. Reaching that goal, however, won't happen by accident. You will need to take purposeful strides to attain it.

This doesn't mean we will be perfect. It doesn't mean that if we sin, we've totally blown it and should just give up. You and I will mess up, perhaps frequently, but that is not the point. The point is that our hearts are never okay with it. We desire to remove sin, seek forgiveness, and start fresh with an attitude that seeks to please our Savior.

Regardless of how you've blown it (or how many times you've done so), never settle for anything less than what God has for you. Never settle for the world's best when you can have God's best. Drive away from the desire for fleeting sin and seek to deepen your relationship with the Creator of the universe.

A ticket to Heaven is not the goal, transformation is.

Time for Transformation

Author and blogger Ethan Renoe tells the story of sitting in a coffee shop one day as a pony-tailed man in a TOOL t-shirt sauntered up to the counter and struck up a conversation with the barista while ordering his preferred caffeine injection.

During the course of that exchange, it somehow came up that she was a student in Bible college. This piqued the interest of the customer, who quickly made it clear that he was not a fan of anything Christian. The "TOOL guy" peppered her with posits, what-ifs, and questions, to which she had few answers. The self-avowed atheist plainly knew more about atheism than the Bible college student knew about Christianity!

With that experience fresh in his brain, Renoe would lament over "a church system which, for the past 200 years, has begun discarding intelligence within the church in favor of emotion, conversion experiences, and passion."

He went on to write, "I'm saddened that atheists are so passionate about what they believe that they will read stacks of books in order to define their beliefs, while we are happy to float along the surface with a (no offense) 'Hillsong-deep theology' and call it good. And we wonder why people are leaving the Church in droves! A church that offers only emotional, squishy feel-good theology is going to lose the long-term wrestling match to a well-read and convincing atheist nearly every time...Just as a marriage cannot be sustained by the tumble of infatuation, a life of faith cannot be sustained by passionate emotion. Yes, it may be a wonderful (and necessary) entryway, but without depth of knowledge and understanding, it will be 'blown here and there by every wind of teaching and by the cunning and craftiness of people in their deceitful scheming' (Ephesians 4:14)."[8]

In Romans 12, Paul gives the prescription for transformation. *Let God transform you into a new person by changing the way you think.*[9] As we've already discussed in this book, it all comes down to what you feed your mind. Instead of feeding on the world and all it offers, we must begin to feed on the things of the Lord.

As we do, there is deepening, maturing, and growth. We begin to think about things the way God thinks about things. We begin to see things the way God sees things. We begin to do things the way God does things. When this happens, the devil's lies are more easily detected, and the world's lures are more easily avoided.

Moreover, as we begin to transform, people start to see Christ in us. When those we encounter have questions, we now have answers. When others need an example to follow, we are able to provide one. And when our friends, relatives, neighbors, work associates, and classmates don't know where to turn, they seek us out because they trust our advice.

Do you want to be that kind of person? If so, adjust your side views once more to get a clear view of what God wants to do in and through your life. Have Bible study and prayer time each day, join a small group, make church a priority, and surround yourself with people who hunger and thirst for more of Christ.

In Hebrews 5, the author of the book tells his readers, *you have been believers so long now that you ought to be teaching others. Instead, you need someone to teach you again the basic things about God's word. You are like babies who need milk and cannot eat solid food. For someone who lives on milk is still an infant and doesn't know how to do what is right. Solid food is for those who are mature, who through training have the skill to recognize the difference between right and wrong.*[10]

When my nephew was one and my son was two, they didn't know much, but they knew how to try and get their way. We should expect nothing less from infants and toddlers. From adults, however, we should expect far more.

Are you ready to grow and mature in the faith?

A lost world that needs desperately to see Christ awaits your answer.

BLIND SPOT
Hell

Roughly ten years ago, while still pastoring in rural Wisconsin, my family had two ferrets named Stinky and Dodger. If you have never owned a ferret, let me tell you that they are pint-sized trouble makers! Those two could climb just about anywhere and seemed to thoroughly enjoy knocking expensive (and breakable) things to the floor.

For fun, they particularly relished tearing into the bottom of our furniture, crawling inside, and refusing to come out. These two-pound critters tormented our sixty-pound dog and stole her food right out of the bowl. Speaking of stealing, our son's stuffed animals, our hats, our car keys, or anything else we happened to leave lying around would often be toted off to Stinky and Dodger's favorite spot…under the guest bed. Yes, they were definitely a handful!

But one Tuesday evening, I noticed Dodger limping. At the time, I didn't think much of it because Stinky and he would occasionally play rough. I figured he must've gotten nipped. By Friday, however, his minor limp had become serious--more dragging than limping. It became clear that a trip to the vet was necessary.

Saturday morning, I woke up early to get Dodger to the

veterinarian before heading to the church. However, when I brought him upstairs and put him down, he could only pull himself across the ground by his front paws. My wife, Christie, audibly gasped when she noticed.

We drove to the local vet, and I left the little guy there with Christie and went to get some work done at the church. During that time, she informed me that Dodger needed to see a specialist in Madison, which was about seventy miles away, so off Christie went to Wisconsin's capital city. In Madison, Dodger underwent a thorough diagnostic, which included X-rays. Those radiographs made it easy to detect a slipped disc that was pressing on a nerve, essentially paralyzing the back half of his body.

There was not much that could be done outside of hoping anti-inflammatory medicine might reduce swelling around the spine and enable the disc to slide back into place. We were told to give pills every twelve hours. Within twenty-four hours, we would know if it was working or not.

The little guy received pill number one around noon, and I set my alarm for midnight to give him another. During this time, Dodger's paralysis didn't just effect his ability to walk, it also affected his ability to control his bladder and bowel movements. This meant he would go to the bathroom on himself and just had to lie in it. I couldn't stand to see that happen.

At midnight, I cleaned him up and gave him fresh bedding. At 6:00 am, before heading to church on Sunday morning, I cleaned him up again and gave him fresh bedding one more time. After church, I repeated the process, then I just sat with him, stroked his back, and started crying...*for a ferret!* At that moment, his brokenness was more than I could take.

A small town being what it is, our veterinarian's office consisted of one vet. I was going to pay whatever necessary to have her come in on a Sunday and end Dodger's misery. Only, she was out of town at a horseshow. It would have to wait until Monday morning.

For the rest of Sunday and into early Monday morning, I cleaned Dodger and his bedding every two hours, even through the night. Finally, at 8:00 am, when the office opened, I took him in. At last, his pain was over.

A Broken World

Later that day, as I sat at home on my day off, the Lord really spoke to me about a few things. He reminded me that over the course of the previous few days, realizing that Dodger was a broken animal, I did everything I could to deal with that brokenness before the end. Knowing that was so, a measure of satisfaction softened the edges of my sadness.

However, then the Lord also reminded me that I live in a broken world filled with broken people. Was I doing everything I could to deal with all of that brokenness? Thinking through that question left me with no measure of satisfaction.

I had spent the previous days grieving over Dodger's condition, and that grief motivated me to action. I knew Dodger's time was short, so I did all I could before the end. Now, there I was hearing the Lord asking some pointed questions, "Why aren't you grieving for the brokenness of My world like you grieved for Dodger? Why aren't you motivated to action over that? And, if you truly believed that Hell is a real place, why aren't you doing all you can so that those around you, still without Christ, won't end up there?" All good questions, for which I had no good answers.

When I returned to church on Tuesday morning, I called a funeral parlor in a neighboring town and asked if I could borrow one of their coffins. The director willingly obliged and dropped one off a few days later. I placed it center stage, right in front of the pulpit.

On Sunday, I shared the following sobering statistics with the congregation. Every day, over 153,000 people die around the world. Breaking that down, close to 6,400 die every hour. That equals nearly 107 a minute (or almost two people every second). In other words, in the time it takes you to read this sentence, eight to ten people around the world will die, two-thirds going into a Christless eternity.

I then opened up the local newspaper, turned to the Obituaries, and read the names of twenty or so individuals. "You know what all those names have in common?" I asked. "What those names have in common is that they all belonged to people who were alive last week, but now are not. One day, one of these names could be a friend, a relative, an associate, a classmate, or a neighbor. One day, you may read their name in this Obituary. Then what will you do when you realize it's too late to bring them to Christ?"

"The fact is," I continued, "sooner or later everyone we know will end up in a coffin. But when their temporal body lies in the coffin, where will their eternal soul be? Make no mistake, Satan is working twenty-four hours a day, seven days a week, 365 days a year to ensure the answer is Hell. How hard are you working to ensure the answer is Heaven?"

Unfortunately, most of us are grieved more by lost pets than lost people, and the reason is we choose to believe that Hell isn't real. Or, if we do believe in Hell, we choose to keep it in our blind spot, so we don't have to think too much about it.

Jesus, however, doesn't allow for either option. No one discusses Hell in the Bible more than Jesus. In fact, He spent more time warning people about the dangers of Hell than He did in comforting them with the hope of Heaven.[1]

Hell is for Real

The Bible does not go into extreme detail about Hell. Moreover, it does not explicitly say what Hell is or how exactly it functions. What the Bible does make clear, however, is that Hell is real and eternal.[2]

Take a few moments to read what Jesus Himself has to say about Hell just from the book of Matthew.

"But I say, if you are even angry with someone, you are subject to judgment! If you call someone an idiot, you are in danger of being brought before the court. And if you curse someone, you are in danger of the fires of hell."[3]

"If your eye—even your good eye—causes you to lust, gouge it out and throw it away. It is better for you to lose one part of your body than for your whole body to be thrown into hell."[4]

"You can enter God's Kingdom only through the narrow gate. The highway to hell is broad, and its gate is wide for the many who choose that way."[5]

"Don't be afraid of those who want to kill your body; they cannot touch your soul. Fear only God, who can destroy both soul and body in hell."[6]

"But many Israelites—those for whom the Kingdom was prepared—will be thrown into outer darkness, where there will be weeping and gnashing of teeth."[7]

"The angels will throw them into the fiery furnace, where there will be weeping and gnashing of teeth."[8]

"That is the way it will be at the end of the world. The angels will come and separate the wicked people from the righteous, throwing the wicked into the fiery furnace, where there will be weeping and gnashing of teeth."[9]

Finally, in Matthew 25, Jesus states, *"But when the Son of Man comes in His glory, and all the angels with Him, then He will sit upon His glorious throne. All the nations will be gathered in His presence, and He will separate them as a shepherd separates the sheep from the goats. He will place the sheep at His right hand and the goats at His left. Then the King will say to those on the right, 'Come, you who are blessed by my Father, inherit the Kingdom prepared for you from the foundation of the world'...Then the King will turn to those on the left and say, 'Away with you, you cursed ones, into the eternal fire prepared for the Devil and his demons!'...And they will go away into eternal punishment, but the righteous will go into eternal life."*[10]

Jesus plainly declares everyone who ever lived will one day stand before Him. At that time, all of humanity will be separated into two groups. On the right will be those who followed Jesus, and on the left will be those who did not.

Imagine what it will be like to stand before the Lord on that day to end all days. What will it be like to stand with those on the right and hear the God of the universe invite you to spend eternity with Him in paradise? It will be unspeakably amazing!

But what if you see a friend, a relative, a classmate, a neighbor, or a work associate standing over on the left? What will it be like to see their horrified faces when Jesus tells them where they are going? What will it be like to hear their agonizing cries, their begging for one final chance?

What will it be like if those people see you over on the right and cry out, "Why didn't you tell me?!? You obviously knew the right way, why didn't you let me know?!?" What will *that* be like? I think it will be unspeakably gut-wrenching.

I guarantee when that day comes, you won't be thinking, "I should have played more golf." "I wish I had played more video games." "I didn't get to watch enough TV." "I should have put another five hours a week in at the office." "Why didn't I earn more money?" "Why didn't I go to the mall more?" "I didn't see all the Marvel movies yet."

No, you won't be thinking like that at all. Instead, you will be grieving all the missed opportunities and all the lost chances. You'll be devastated by the fact that you left the truth of Hell in your blind spot and kept on driving down the road of life without even giving eternity a second thought.

We can no longer afford to keep the truth of Hell in our blind spot. Instead, we must live each day as though Christ will come back the next. How our lives would change if we believed the Lord was returning in a mere twenty-four hours!

Would you want your last day of conversations to be about the weather or about whether or not someone was saved and ready for eternity? Would you want your last stories to be about how some Marvel movie character saved the day or about how Jesus saved the world? Would you want the last songs people hear you singing to be about shapes of bodies and butterfly wings or about our beautiful Savior? Would you want your last evening to be spent with video games and broadcast TV or with broken people who need to experience the Healer before the next day is over?

If you truly believe in the existence of Hell, the above questions should be easy to answer.

None Left Behind

In my book *World Changer,* I ask readers to picture a couple out camping with their five children. No, I don't know why they're camping either. My feeling is if God had intended for people to sleep in tents, He wouldn't have invented houses. And let's not even talk about the bathrooms, or lack thereof, at a campground…but I digress.

Back to the couple camping with their five children. Thinking he heard a noise, Dad wakes up in the middle of the night. As he groggily scans the tent, he notices that all the kids' sleeping bags are empty.

Unzipping the tent and peering out, he sees the charred remains of their evening campfire, but no sign of his children anywhere. Getting worried, he awakens his wife. The pair hurriedly grab some flashlights and begin searching the woods, shouting out in the darkness for their lost children.

After what seems like forever, the sun slowly pulls itself above the horizon, bringing with it the light of dawn. Yet, there is still no sign of the kids. Mom, in desperation mode, races back to the tent to grab her cellphone and call 9-1-1.

While she's in mid-dial, though, Dad comes running back with one of the children and motions for her to hang up. "Don't worry honey, I found one! No need to bother the police now. One kid is good enough. Let's just pack up and leave."

Mom protests, "Pack up and leave!?! We should at least find one more. I'm not leaving until we've found two of our five children!"

A few minutes later, another child is found happily playing with coyotes in poison ivy. Rejoicing, the now jubilant parents grab their gear, put their two children in the car, and head home, stopping for ice-cream on the way.

Could such a story ever be true? Would this couple really settle for just two out of five children? Would they actually leave three children lost in the woods? Absolutely not! Those parents would not rest nor stop searching until *all* their children were found, for they know that lost children could end up dead children.

God is no different. He is not satisfied with small percentages and handfuls of salvations. He would not have us stop until the whole world hears the message of salvation. Why? Because lost people end up dead people. And dead people without Jesus end up in Hell.

The day will come when there will be no more time for seeking and no more time for saving. One day it will be too late. What we do until that day will literally make an eternal difference. How do you plan on spending the time between now and then?

As we discussed earlier, over 153,000 people around the world die every day. This means, in one year, roughly fifty-six million will die, and within six years the equivalent of the population of the United States will be dead.

Where will they be?

From Hell to Heaven

There's a story of two young brothers, one nine and the other seven, who decided that they would go exploring in the woods around their new home. These boys were excited about their plans and spent most of the morning making the equipment they would need to do the best exploring. Older brother made a pair binoculars out of construction paper and also drew himself a compass.

Meanwhile, younger brother tried to make a canteen out of construction paper, but soon discovered that construction paper doesn't hold water very well. Armed with that knowledge, he decided it was best to ask Mom if he could borrow the water bottle she used while riding her stationary bike.

Soon the boys were ready to begin. Before they left, however, Dad gathered his sons together and told them, "You can go anywhere in the woods around our backyard, but stay out of the clearing!"

The boys agreed to the boundaries then raced off into the woods. Their exploratory trip was a blast as they checked out bird's nests, squirrel holes, and more. Running through the trees, they ducked under low branches, swung on high ones, and reconnoitered all over the place…and then came to the clearing. It was a strange looking clearing, as all the ground seemed to slope toward the center.

They remembered Dad's words and knew they shouldn't enter but did anyway. As they moved slowly toward the center of the clearing, the ground gave way. Waves of fear swept over them, their stomachs soared to their throats, as they dropped twenty-five feet to the soggy ground below.

The nine year-old hit first, shattering his left leg. Little brother crashed to the ground shoulder first, separating the ball from the socket. The pain for both was excruciating. Scared, hurting, and unsure of what had happened, the boys cried out in panic. They were effectively trapped in a dark and shadowy place with no way out.

Moreover, the base of the pit was eight to ten inches of a gooey, sticky mud that virtually encased the boys. Trying to pull their feet and hands free was like trying to free themselves from wet cement. They could barely move--their bodies stuck in a thick blanket of mud.

It seemed a hopeless situation.

Scared and badly hurt, there was no way they could free themselves. No matter what they tried, it proved useless. The only way to be freed from their dark, miry prison was for help to come from above. Sure enough, when the boys hadn't come home, Dad went looking for them. He soon heard his sons' screams for help. Minutes later, help indeed came from above. A rescuer was sent down to pull them both up.

Now consider this. In the beginning, Father God gave us a world to explore, but He also gave us boundaries. We all too quickly discarded Dad's boundaries and soon found ourselves trapped in sin. Trapped with no way to save ourselves. Caught in a prison of sin and self, there was no way out. The situation was dire. The only hope was help from above.

And that's exactly what we got.

The Lord heard the screams of His lost and trapped children, so He sent a rescuer down. Indeed, Jesus came down in order to pull us up. Just as those two boys were stuck in a mud-filled shaft, so we are stuck in sin, trapped by our own wrong choices with no hope of freeing ourselves.

Without a doubt, all of us have said bad things, done bad things, and thought bad things. Each one of those things is called "sin." Sin separates us from a relationship with God, and we can't do anything about it. There is no cure within ourselves for sin. Just as those two boys could only be freed by a rescuer from above, so we too could only be freed from our sin that same way.

John 3:16 says, *for this is how God loved the world: He gave his one and only Son, so that everyone who believes in him will not perish but have eternal life.*

The Bible tells us that God loved us so much that He sent a rescuer down to free us from our sin. He sent His Son Jesus to come and die in our places, for our sins, so that we could have forgiveness and eternal life.

1 John 1:9 tells us that *if we confess our sins to him, he is faithful and just to forgive us our sins and to cleanse us from all wickedness.*

To be freed from our bondage we need only cry out, "God, I have sinned. I have said and thought and done bad things, but I believe you sent Jesus to free me from my sins. Please forgive me." Those words will lift us up out of the miry clay and put us on dry land. More than that, God will come and fill us with assurance. We are now His children and Heaven is ours.

But what about the others still stuck in the pit? What about those still trapped in sin and lost in darkness? What will be their fate if we don't let them know of the Rescuer who came, died, and rose again to set them free?

The answer: Their fate is eternal separation from God in a place the Bible calls Hell, and whether or not we leave this fact stuck in our blind spot doesn't make it any less true. That means, before the end, we have work to do. And it's time to get started.

Not sure how? Well, on that Sunday after Dodger's death, I handed everyone in my church a card with five lines on it. I told them to write down the names of five people—friends, relatives, classmates, coworkers, neighbors—who needed to know Jesus as their Lord and Savior. After writing those names down, they were told to commit to praying for those people *every day*, asking the Lord to work in their hearts and to provide opportunities to share the Good News.

If you are looking for a place to start, I would suggest the same to you. Write down the names of five unsaved people that you have regular contact with. Pray for those individuals every day and seek opportunities to show them Christ.

On that last day, when the sheep and goats are separated, they will be eternally grateful that you did.

BLIND SPOT
The Spiritual Battle

As I write this, I am in my mid-forties.

Depending on your age, you may have just read that and thought, "You're old!" Or, "Oh, to be that young again!" Regardless, whatever way you look at it, I think I am old enough now to start using this phrase: "I never thought I'd see the day."

Of course, I never thought I'd see the day when I would start saying, "I never thought I'd see the day." But let me give you a few examples. For instance, I never thought I'd see the day when *I* was the uncool or embarrassing one.

Parents and grandparents out there, do you remember when you were the cool ones? And then, all of sudden, someone comes along, with your last name and *much* younger than you, and declares that you are no longer cool. In fact, not only aren't you cool, you don't even know what cool is!

I also never thought I'd never see the day when I needed a helper to drive my car. But since I am getting older, and am married, I have a helper while driving. She lets me know how fast I am going, "Do you know how fast you're going?"

"Yeah, I have a speedometer right in front of me. Thanks."

She lets me know when the traffic light turns colors and everything. "It's green you know."

"Thanks Captain Colorwheel, I got it."

And if all that wasn't bad enough, a couple months ago while getting my haircut, the stylist was like, "Your highlights are incredible. Who does your highlights? You know I do highlights and I never get them this good. The way they blend…." She was going on and on.

Finally, I had to say, "Those aren't highlights. That's gray hair." I never thought I'd see the day when someone thought I had highlights because of all my gray!

Worse Days Ahead
Of course, those kinds of "I never thought I'd see the day" stories are humorous. However, I have some other such stories that aren't nearly so funny. For example, one day while my son was having his guitar lesson at a local lesson center, I sat in the waiting area perusing a magazine.

There was a section in the magazine that was all about "Must See Season Finales." One of these "Must See Finales" involved a show where the whole plot line revolved around a teenage boy going to buy a ring for his boyfriend. Well, I never thought I'd see the day when that was must see TV.

In my state of Pennsylvania, the Haverford Township School District refused to allow Child Evangelism Fellowship to participate in its flier distribution program. They allowed the Cub Scouts, Boy/Girl Scouts, the YMCA, and various other community organizations to participate, but not CEF.[1]

Moreover, in Colorado, Monarch High School refused to allow students to form a Bible club, yet the school has a Gay-Alliance, a peace club, and a multicultural club.[2] In Connecticut, Federal Judge Janet Hall ruled that two Enfield high schools could not hold their graduations inside a local church, stating that the schools were coercing the students "to support religion by forcing them to enter a church for graduation."[3]

The Pattison Elementary School in Katy, Texas banned the singing of all Christian Christmas carols and then threatened to lower the grades of any student who refused to participate in the secular Christmas program.[4] At Northwest Elementary in Massachusetts, a second grade student brought the book *The First Christmas* to fulfill an assignment about her family's Christmas traditions. She was forbidden to share her book because it was about Jesus being born.[5]

Similarly, a second-grader in the Frenchtown, New Jersey school district was denied the right to sing the song "Awesome God" for her school's talent show. The school district went so far as to serve her family with a temporary restraining order which barred the performance at "Frenchtown Idol."[6]

It doesn't end there. In Alaska public schools, students were told they could not use the word "Christmas" in school because it had the word "Christ" in it, nor could they have the word in their notebooks, nor exchange Christmas cards or presents, nor display anything with the word "Christmas" on it.[7]

Meanwhile, the Postmaster of Appleton, Wisconsin invited students from area schools to submit artwork for display at the local post office. However, when the students at Appleton Christian School were selected to submit their artwork, a postal employee advised them "to avoid decorations that are overly religious." They were later told they could not include manger scenes or the word "Christmas" on their greeting card art.[8]

I learned about the Santa Clara school district in Florida which banned voluntary, student-initiated prayers, off the clock discussions about religion, and the use of the phrase "God Bless."[9] And finally, I read about Federal Judge Robert Gettleman who banned moments of silence in the state of Illinois stating that "it was a subtle attempt to force children at impressionable ages to contemplate religion."[10] Did you ever think you'd see the day?

This is our culture now. This is the day we live in. A day when a battle rages between good and evil for the hearts and minds of every American. If our country is going to make its way back to God, it is going to take us opening our eyes to reality of what is going on all around us.

There's No Compromise in War
In 1 Peter 5:8, we read, *stay alert! Watch out for your great enemy, the devil. He prowls around like a roaring lion, looking for someone to devour.* When a lion is attacking, there is no stopping to reason with it or hold out for some sort of compromise.

"Hey, how about I let you chew off my left foot, and we'll call it even?" Sorry, that's not happening. You run for your life or stand and fight with all the strength you can muster. Similarly, when it comes to the devil and his attacks, the Bible allows no room for compromise. Verse 9 continues, *stand firm against him, and be strong in your faith.*

I'd like to look at what Jesus says about this in the book of Revelation. Before I do, however; you'll need a little background information from the book of Numbers. There, we encounter a couple of sketchy guys named Balak and Balaam. The Israelites at that time were about to head into the Promised Land. The Midianites, who were living in that area already, were scared. Out of this fear, the king of the Midianites, Balak, attempted to hire the prophet Balaam to curse the Israelites, hoping that God would destroy the whole lot of them so they couldn't threaten his people.

However, Numbers 24:1 tells us that Balaam knew full well that God wanted to bless the Israelites, so he couldn't just get God to wipe them all out with a curse. He had to do something more subtle. Something so subtle, in fact, we don't actually find out what he did until seven chapters later.

In Numbers 31, we discover that Balaam's solution was to get the Israelites to compromise. He essentially told King Balak, "Follow this plan. Get the Israelites to join you at your festivals, get them to follow your customs, get them to marry your women, get them to build families with your people, then you won't need worry about them at all. They won't be a threat to you because they will be like you."

Satan, much like Balaam, knows that God wants very much to bless His people, us. This means, he further knows that he can't wipe us off the map and end the threat we are to his battle plans. So what can he do? He can get us to compromise--to join in with the culture, to become like it--so we are not a threat to it.

His goal: Get us to watch what they watch, do what they do, listen to what they listen to, speak like they speak, think like they think, etc.

From Numbers, flash forward fifteen hundred years and head to the book of Revelation. There, Jesus tells the church at Pergamum, *"I have a few complaints against you. You tolerate some among you whose teaching is like that of Balaam, who showed Balak how to trip up the people of Israel. He taught them to sin by eating food offered to idols and by committing sexual sin. In a similar way, you have some Nicolaitans among you who follow the same teaching."[11]*

Jesus bluntly points out to this first century church, "The same thing that Satan did through Balaam and Balak back in Numbers is happening today, fifteen hundred years later, with you!" Only, in the first century, it was happening through a group of people known as the Nicolaitans.

What's a Nicolaitan, you ask? Well, according to one Bible commentary, they were "believers who compromised their faith to enjoy the practices of [their] society."[12] Compromisers. The devil used them when God's people first planned to take the Promised Land, and fifteen centuries later, compromisers haven't gone anywhere. Tack on nineteen hundred more years to today, and the temptation to compromise still exists.

If Satan can get us to compromise with the culture, we won't be a threat to his battle plans, evil will push forward, and Hell will continue to fill. Instead of fighting against the devil, compromise causes us to flow right along with him and the culture. Indeed, compromise is a killer to the kingdom of God--which is precisely why Jesus *hates* it.

"Whoa, hold on, Mark. There you go using strong words again." You're right. Hate is a strong word, and it's used by Christ in Revelation 2:6, *"This is in your favor: You hate the evil deeds of the Nicolaitans, just as I do."* In other words, Jesus is saying, "This is what I like about you. You *hate* compromise as much as I do!"

And why does God hate compromise? Because if you

compromise on one thing, it's not that much further until it's two, three, four, or more things. For example, in 1981, Charles Rocket used a particular curse word on *Saturday Night Live* and was fired that same week. Last year, that same word was heard over a thousand times on over 180 programs without any issues. The same is true in our lives. One thing leads to two, two leads to four, four leads to...well, you get the idea.

Think about this—if I gave a thirty minute sermon at your church and used ten curse words, many of your fellow church members would probably be upset. I, most likely, would be sandblasted off the short list of future guest speakers. Yet, if you hear the same amount of cursing on a thirty minute sit-com, you may not even think twice about it. What's the difference?

The difference is this. As we discussed in the chapter on entertainment choices, we have compromised so much in this area that we don't think twice about it. But I tell you, if it is condemned in the Bible and considered wrong for a sermon, then it is wrong in the movie theater, wrong on the TV in your living room, wrong on your lips, and wrong in your heart.

Your Legacy

In the book *UnChristian* the Christian Research Group— Barna "found that [in 28] lifestyle activities, born-again Christians were *statistically equivalent* to those of non-born agains. When asked to identify their activities over the last thirty days, born again believers were *just as likely* to gamble, visit a pornographic website, take something that didn't belong to them, consult a psychic, fight or abuse someone, consume enough alcohol to be legally drunk, to use illegal, nonprescription drugs, to lie, to get back at someone, and to have said mean things behind someone else's back" (emphasis mine).[13]

This is exactly what Balaam hoped would happen when he told King Balak, "Just invite them to your festivals, encourage participation in your events, introduce their men to your women, let them start families together, then you won't need to worry about them. They won't be a threat to you because they will be like you."

Today, roughly 3500 years after Balaam, Christians are statistically no different from the culture. And this all starts in the home with the little choices we make: What to watch, what to listen to, what to read, how to spend our free time. What movies are in our DVD collection; what songs are on our mp3 players; what TV shows do we watch; what books do we read; how do we handle problems that arise in the house; what desires are in our hearts; what thoughts are in our minds? Does it all conform to Scripture or to culture?

I hope you understand. There is a real battle going on for the hearts and minds of every man, woman, and child that surrounds your life. As we discussed in the last chapter, Satan is actively and intentionally fighting to lead people away from the truth and toward Hell. This means we all need to be asking ourselves, "How actively and intentionally am I seeking to live, think, speak, and act like Christ, so that people can see His difference in me and encounter Him because of it?"

Eternity is potentially riding on our answer. A Christ-like legacy can greatly increase the chances of a heavenly eternity for our friends, relatives, associates, classmates, and neighbors, but the opposite is also true. If we blend in with the culture, those God has placed around us won't see a reflection of Christ (only a reflection of the culture). That reality has eternal ramifications.

We know that the culture is not going to correct itself. It is going to take us, the body of Christ, to go out and be Christ's hands and feet. To be His love and His holiness. To say "Yes" to what honors Him and to say "No" to what does not. To live in such a way that, when those in the culture look at us, they see Christ reflected and not themselves.

In the 1500s, a stubborn (and chubby) priest named Martin Luther decided he was going to live a different kind of life—one that honored Christ and His Word above anyone and anything else. This choice got him in serious straights with the two most powerful people of his day—the Holy Roman Emperor and the Pope. As he stood before Emperor Charles V and the pope's representatives on April 18, 1521, he was told in no uncertain terms to knock it off or face serious consequences (like a potential date with a burning stake). Luther, though, was not dissuaded. He famously responded, "I am subject to God's Word. I cannot and will not recant. Here I stand. I can do no other."

His response recalls the words of the Apostle Paul, *put on every piece of God's armor so you will be able to resist the enemy in the time of evil. Then after the battle you will still be standing firm. Stand your ground...*[14]

Today, I encourage you to stand your ground as well. Refuse to compromise. Base *all* of your life choices on God's Word not just select parts of it. Stand on the Word of God and do no other. Fight the good fight and never surrender.

Did You Just Say Fight?

I have a sister who is two and a half years younger than me. When we were young, my family took many trips by car. In fact, we went by car to all of our vacation destinations. There were no flights for the Musser family. This meant *lots* of time in the car with this sister of mine, Stephanie. Now I know this might cause some of you to shudder, but we actually had to take these hours' long trips without I-phones, I-pads, portable DVD players, etc. Those things did not exist.

What existed was a little magnetic checkers game and the alphabet game. Anyone else remember being so eye-numbingly bored that you played the alphabet game? You know the game where you would have to find a road sign that had a word starting with the letter "A," then the letter "B" and so on. You'd breeze along through a bunch of letters and then be stuck on "Q" for two hours. Yeah, it was great.

Well, as we vainly sought a word starting with "Q", we would often fight. "She's touching me."

"He's looking out my window!"

"What do you mean 'your window'? You don't have your own window. They're everyone's windows."

Back and forth and back and forth...until dad broke out those dreaded words, "If I have to pull this car over, you'll both be sorry." Sadly, I must confess, a couple times the car did get pulled over, and "unpleasantness" ensued.

Of course, after all the unpleasantness, there would be a lecture on how fighting is not the answer. There were better ways to solve problems, and Jesus wanted us to all get along and not fight. You probably heard similar lectures. After all, haven't most of us been taught at one time or another not to fight? Yet, here I am telling you it's time to start fighting. In fact, more than that, I am *encouraging* you to do so and to never, ever stop. So let's try to make some sense of this.

Fighting for your selfish wants, fighting to defend your selfish desires and pursuits, all of that is wrong. However, to fight with your life, to defend a cause, to gird up for battle so you can stand for truth, now that *is* good fighting, the kind God expects from all of His children. We are, remember, in a war.

Ephesians 6:12 clearly states, *we are not fighting against flesh-and-blood enemies, but against evil rulers and authorities of the unseen world, against mighty powers in this dark world, and against evil spirits in the heavenly places.*

Yes, we are in a war. A real-life battle for the hearts, minds, and souls of every man, woman, and child on this planet. And, praise the Lord, in some parts of the world, this battle is being won by God's faithful people. Sadly, in America, we are losing. Badly.

If fact, the very non-Christian Bill Maher, on his popular talk show, posted the video of Michael Sam (who is black and the first openly gay football player to be drafted into the NFL) kissing his white boyfriend after hearing he was selected by the Dolphins. Citing this inter-racial gay kiss, Maher pronounced. "The culture war is over, and we won!"[15] To back that up, after a Dolphins player tweeted his disappointment, he was immediately suspended by the Dolphins, fined, and told he could not return to the team until he underwent sensitivity training.[16]

Listen, I am a competitive guy, who *really* doesn't like to lose, so I would love to type that we are winning the fight, but that would be a lie. Since that is the case, I wanted to finish this book with a challenge for you to fight and fight hard. While praying about exactly how to do that, God reminded me of Admiral McRaven.

Don't Ring the Bell
Admiral McRaven, a Navy Seal for thirty-six years, gave a commencement address at the University of Texas a few years

back.[17] As he spoke, he shared with the students ten ways to change the world. It is the last of those ten that I want to focus on. *Don't ring the bell.*

To understand what that means, you have to understand Navy Seal training. It is perhaps the most intense there is. To be part of that elite fighting unit, you need to outlast six punishing months of brutal qualification training—training that taxes the limits of your physical, mental, and emotional capacities.

This training, however, is not a prison. You see, there is a bell that goes along with the Navy Seal candidates to every exercise they are put through. Should a candidate wish to quit, all he (or she) need do is ring the bell. Ringing the bell announces that you have quit. You have given up and surrendered. Your training is over. Your chance to be a Seal, done.

Who could blame people for wanting to ring that bell? Seal qualification training is twenty-six weeks of long torturous runs in soft sand, midnight swims in frigid water, obstacles courses filled with jagged barbed wire, unending calisthenics, days without sleep, and almost always being cold, wet, and miserable.

The ninth week of training is referred to as "Hell Week." It is six days of virtually no sleep, constant physical and mental harassment, and one special day at the Mud Flats. The Flats is an area between San Diego and Tijuana where water runs off to create what is known as the Tijuana slue—a swampy patch of terrain where the muck effectively engulfs you. On Wednesday of Hell Week, trainees paddle down to the Flats and spend the next fifteen hours trying to survive the freezing cold mud, the howling wind, and the incessant pressure to quit from instructors. (Sounds like a marriage seminar my wife wanted me to go to once!)

But it can all be over with one ring of that brass bell. Ring the bell and you no longer have to wake up before the sun. Ring the bell and you no longer have to do the freezing cold swims. Ring the bell and you no longer have to do the runs, the obstacle course, or anything else. Just ring the bell and you can leave the fight. Though, if you ring the bell, you won't ever become a Seal.

As Admiral McRaven challenged the graduates of UT, I want to challenge you. Do *not* ring the bell. Do *not* choose the easy road. Choose the hard road and the narrow way. When you are tempted to flow along with the culture and give up the fight, remember that if you want to change the world for Jesus Christ, you can never, ever ring that bell.

Please know that I am not trying to offend you, but given the state of things in America, I'll chance it by saying many of us have already rung the bell. When we choose to ignore or excuse sin in entertainment, the bell has been rung and a battle lost. Certainly, entertaining ourselves to death while the culture falls apart is not part of God's good, perfect, and pleasing plan for us.

When we choose to gossip or don't confront gossip in the church, we ring the bell. When we surf porn or do nothing to help the church confront the issue of porn, we ring the bell. When we content ourselves with our spiritual condition and don't seek deeper Christ-likeness, we ring the bell. When we treat sin as something to be played with in moderate doses, we ring the bell. When we act as though Hell doesn't exist and spend our days wrapped up in our own pursuits, we ring the bell. And, certainly, when we close our eyes to the battle raging around us because we don't want to make waves or leave our comfort zone, we ring the bell.

Don't ring the bell!

In John Bunyon's classic work, *Pilgrim's Progress*, Pilgrim starts out on his journey with a guy named Pliable. Now, Pliable hears about all the great things that God has waiting for him in the Celestial City, so he excitedly joins Pilgrim on this quest. However, they soon get to a sludge-filled bog. The going is slowed and slogging through the muck proves hard and dirty work.

Pliable's initial excitement rapidly fades, and he basically tells Christian, "I thought this was going to be a great adventure where we would get all this amazing stuff from God. I didn't know it was going to be hard. I didn't know I was going to get dirty. If this is what it is like now, what will it be like later?"[18] And he turns around and goes home. He rings the bell. He leaves the fight.

To change the world for Jesus Christ, you can't ring the bell. You can't expect it to be easy, to be fun, to be just as you want it to be. It won't! It will require, as it does for Navy Seals, dedication, commitment, and resolve.

Dedicating Yourself to the Fight
Not ringing the bell means that you get up thirty minutes before you have to because you want to dig into the Word before work or school. It means taking your face off a screen—whether it be an I-pod, I-phone, laptop, TV, or movie screen—and instead go face to face with the God of the universe in prayer to intercede for friends, relatives, associates, classmates, and neighbors; for politicians, for Hollywood, for our culture, and for so much more.

Don't ring the bell. Don't choose the easy way. It is hard to read the Bible every morning when you could sleep in longer. It is hard to pray for thirty minutes straight when it seems there is so much to watch or to do, but we are in a fight. We are in a war. It's time to do hard things. It's time to say, "I will not ring the bell. I will fight! I will fill my heart with God's Word, not the culture's entertainment. I will go face to face with God instead of burying my face in a screen. I will involve myself in missions and service and bless others instead of expecting everyone to bless me. I won't ring the bell. I won't ever ring the bell."

In the summer of 1940, the Germans were poised to strike Great Britain. World War II had begun. Germany destroyed Poland in three weeks, stormed across Belgium in six days, and crushed France in forty days. Britain was the only major threat left. Knowing a momentous battle that could change the course of the world was looming, Winston Churchill addressed Great Britain on June 4th, 1940.

As his voice crackled over the radio, this is what the British people heard. "Even though large tracts of Europe and many old and famous States have fallen or may fall into the grip of the Gestapo and all the odious apparatus of Nazi rule, we shall not flag or fail. We shall go on to the end. We shall fight in France, we shall fight on the seas and oceans; we shall fight with growing confidence and growing strength in the air. We shall defend our island, whatever the cost may be. We shall fight on the beaches; we shall fight on the landing grounds; we shall fight in the fields and in the streets; we shall fight in the hills; we shall never surrender."

Two weeks later, on June 18th, 1940, the battle for Britain was looming ever nearer. As the people of London were urged to head into bunkers, Churchill spoke again. "But if we fail, then the whole world…will sink into the abyss of a new dark age made more sinister…Let us therefore brace ourselves to our duties, and so bear ourselves, that if the British Empire and its Commonwealth last for a thousand years, men will still say, 'This was their finest hour.'"

As those words still ring in your consciousness, let me finish with this. I don't know how long America has left. But if it is to last one thousand more years, I want us to live and fight for Christ in such a way that people ten centuries from now will say this was our finest hour. We were the generation that changed the world.

I pray we will be that generation. Yet, to be that generation, we must never, ever ring the bell. We must fight the good fight, finish the race, and remain faithful.

Are you in?

EPILOGUE
Stop Thinking for Yourself

Not too long ago I sat in deep conversation with a college-aged student. Having known this young man since he was eleven years-old, I had noticed, over the preceding few years, how his decisions and choices were moving farther and farther from the evangelical mooring he had received from his faith-filled parents.

Questioning him on this, he simply replied, "I've learned to think for myself."

We continued our conversation for a few more minutes, then parted. Afterwards, I could not shake the conservation from my mind, specifically his "I've learned to think for myself" comment. The more I thought about his words, the stranger they seemed to me.

I wondered, "Isn't stating 'I learned to think for myself' kind of like saying, 'I've learned to breathe for myself'?" Do you really need to learn to think for yourself? It seems such thinking comes as naturally as breathing. In fact, there is really no *learning* involved at all. You just do it.

Consider the following. Some months back, I was at a

playground with a friend of mine and his two year-old son, Luke, who wanted desperately to get his tiny body to the top of a massive three-section playset.

The first section, farthest right, was a platform from which kids could scoot down two plastic slides. Connecting this section to the middle section was a rope bridge that seemed to scream at my friend, Scott, "I am doom to your toddler!" Because of this, Scott was not so keen on his young child making his way to the playset.

Nevertheless, Luke persisted. Finally, Dad relented. "You can go up there but *only to go down the slide.*" Luke nodded and my friend lifted him up onto the platform. In the blink of an eye, the little guy made a beeline for the rope bridge. Moving in quickly, Scott grabbed his mischievous boy and whisked him off the platform.

"I told you that you could only go down the slide!" My pal strongly reminded the toddler in a firm voice.

"Okay, slide," Luke muttered back.

"Daddy is serious," Scott continued, "You can *only* go down the slide. Don't go near those ropes."

"Okay, slide," the boy muttered again, this time with a nod.

At that, my frazzled friend hoisted his boy back onto the platform and started moving toward the end of the slide to catch Luke. Luke, however, had other plans. As soon as Dad stepped away, he bolted for the rope bridge again as fast as his wobbly legs would carrying him!

Scott instantly leapt toward Luke and pulled him from the platform just before he hit the rope bridge. Needless to say, the boy did *not* get a third chance.

Did you catch what was happening in Luke's toddler-sized brain in the above story? Even though his mind was not well-developed enough to compose full sentences, still it could form the thought, "What lie can I tell Daddy to get me up on that platform? Oh, I know, 'okay, slide.'" Indeed, anyone who has parented a toddler can tell you that no one needs to teach a young child to think for himself. It comes all too naturally.

You see, our need is *not* learning to think for ourselves. No. Our need is learning to *stop* thinking for ourselves and to start thinking like Christ. Truly, any toddler can think for himself, but it takes a mature and purposeful Christian to begin thinking like the Lord.

The Mind of Christ
Why do we hold grudges instead of forgiving? Because we think for ourselves and not like Christ.

Why do we linger on a lustful thought instead of casting it aside? Because we think for ourselves and not like Christ.

Why do we get mad at another's miniscule faults but excuse our major ones? Because we think for ourselves and not like Christ.

Why do we put our wants above the needs of others? Because we think for ourselves and not like Christ.

Why do we spend hours surfing the internet or playing video games but can't find the time to study Scripture and pray? Because we think for ourselves and not like Christ.

Why do we gossip about others instead of going directly to the person we have an issue with? Because we think for ourselves and not like Christ?

Why do we watch movies and TV shows filled with things the Bible calls sinful, yet we call it entertainment? Because we think for ourselves and not like Christ.

Why is it that we can talk to people about sports and weather and school and politics but can't seem to ever talk about our Christian faith? Because we think for ourselves and not like Christ.

Why do we keep stuff in our blind spots instead of confronting and dealing with it all? Because we think for ourselves and not like Christ?

Oh, the list can go on and on. But, in the end, it all comes down to this. To truly live out the good, pleasing, and perfect plan the Lord has for each of us, we must stop thinking for ourselves and start thinking like Christ.

We can no longer allow the culture, the crowd, or our conscience to be our guide. Christ must be our guide, and He must govern all our thoughts. 1 Corinthians tells us that we are to have the mind of Christ.[1] Meanwhile, the book of Romans implores us to allow God to transform us by changing the way we think.[2]

In Philippians 2:5, we are called to *have the same attitude that Jesus Christ had.* In the original Greek, the word for "attitude" literally means "set your mind." In other words, this passage is basically saying, "Set your mind to the mind of Jesus Christ."

Such a setting of the mind does not happen by accident nor at once. It involves purposeful, and moment by moment, decisions to stop thinking for ourselves and to allow Christ to shape and mold our every thought. As the apostle Paul says in 2 Corinthians, we are to capture all our rebellious thoughts and teach them to obey Christ.[3]

The word *Christian*, after all, means "Christ-one" or "one who is like Christ." Therefore, it is the goal of each and every one us who identifies as a follower of Christ to become more and more like Him. So that, in the end, we can all say along with Paul, *My old self has been crucified with Christ. It is no longer I who live, but Christ lives in me. So I live in this earthly body by trusting in the Son of God, who loved me and gave himself for me.*[4]

My prayer is that this book has moved you one step closer to that reality.

GOD BLESS!

STUDY GUIDE

STUDY QUESTIONS
Sin

Ice Breakers
What do you believe the average person in our culture thinks about the concept of "sin"?

What do you believe the average evangelical Christian in our culture thinks about the concept of "sin"?

Chapter Study
There were several Scripture references in Chapter One which clearly stated that God *hates* sin. The word used for *hate* in many of those verses can best be translated *detestable enmity*. Knowing this, how does the Bible describe God's view of sin?

In the chapter, we read, "The Second Member of the Trinity takes our sin upon Himself. Our sin that God truly and totally detests; yes, our sin that God has made His enemy. In His hatred for this sin, God rips Himself from His earthly communion with Christ. Experiencing this disunion for the first time since before there was time, Jesus cries out, 'My God, my God, why have you forsaken me?'" With these words in mind, how is the cross a stunning object lesson for what we should do with any sin in our lives?

Read: Romans 8:12-13; Colossians 3:5-8; Galatians 5:24-25…What do these verses say we should do with sin in our lives?

In what areas of your life are you struggling to "put sin to death"?

Whenever someone talks about removing certain things from their lives (thoughts, entertainment choices, places frequented, certain individuals, etc.), someone usually comes along to complain about "legalism." However, according to Jesus in Luke 6:46-49 (as well John 14:15, 23-24; 15:14), why is following Scriptural commands *not* legalistic?

Ephesians 4:30 states, *do not bring sorrow to God's Holy Spirit by the way you live.* The word used for sorrow in that verse literally means *pain or anguish.* When we sin, more than just upsetting the Lord, we actually grieve His Spirit. How should such a thought change the way we look at sin, and the way we think about our sinful choices?

Before reading Chapter 1, had you considered how your choices affected God's Spirit? If not, how has this chapter opened your eyes to this reality?

Application Questions

Did your own view of sin change while reading the chapter? If not, why not? If so, what changed?

Earlier, we asked in what areas of your life are you struggling to "put sin to death." With those areas in mind, talk through what might need to change so that those sins no longer negatively effect your life?

Are there areas where accountability might help? If so, think about who can be an accountability partner for you. Having someone committed to praying for you, as well as willing to ask the tough questions when necessary, is a tremendous asset for anyone seeking to put sin to death.

Close in prayer

STUDY QUESTIONS
Gossip

Ice Breakers

Share an experience from a time when words really impacted your life positively?

Share an experience from a time when words really impacted your life negatively?

Chapter Study

Read: Psalm 141:3; Proverbs 10:19-21, 18:19-21; James 1:26...In these Scripture references, what does the Bible say about the tongue?

Read: James 3:1-6. Why do you think that James is so graphic in his description of the tongue?

In Chapter 2, you read, "In the Hebrew mindset, when you spoke a word, you actually created a living thing. Just as God brought life and creation into existence through His word, so the Hebrews believed that when your breath pushed words past your lips, life came forth. And, sometimes, that life caused death to the listener." How does understanding this mindset play into James description of the tongue?

A University of Denver study followed couples for their first ten years of marriage. They found that those couples which divorced within those ten years used two to five times as many negative words with each other. Studies have also shown that children who receive a majority of negative comments from their parents are much less emotionally stable and more likely to engage in risky behaviors than children who receive more positive words. How do these studies further emphasize the power of words and the tongue?

In the New Testament Greek, the word for *gossip* can literally be translated as *whisper lies* or *slander in secret*. In the Old Testament, the Hebrew word for *gossip* means *scandal monger* or *merchant of tales*. How do such translations make it hard to discount gossip as a "little sin"?

What is the best way to handle a situation when you hear someone gossiping?

Read: Ephesians 4:29-32. What does God call us to do with our words?

Application Questions

On a scale from one to ten, with one being "mostly negative" and ten being "mostly positive," rate the way you generally speak to others. Explain your rating.

Based on your rating, what may need to change?

Having you been guilty of gossip in your family, church, and/or community? If so, what must you do to make amends?

How can you practice helpful and encouraging speech?

At the end of Chapter 2, it was suggested that you ask yourself the following questions before speaking: Is it true? It is helpful? Is it inspiring? Is it necessary? Is it kind? How can reviewing these questions help you better guard your tongue going forward?

Close in Prayer

STUDY QUESTIONS
The Fear of the Lord

Ice Breakers

When you hear the word *fear,* what usually comes to mind?

Are there things, issues, critters, etc. that you have a legitimate fear of? If so, what?

How is the fear of the Lord different from the above fears you may have mentioned?

Chapter Study

In Chapter 3, we looked at several studies which showed that children who grow up with parents that combine both "high love" and "high discipline" have the best chance of becoming healthy, well-adjusted adults. Yet, when it comes to Father God, our culture seems to view Him as an indulgent parent who has lost the "high discipline" and only engages in "high love." Why do you think this is so?

Review one or more of the following stories from the Bible: Genesis 3; Deuteronomy 3:23-29; Joshua 7:19-26; 2 Samuel

12, and Acts 5:1-11. In these stories, how do we see that our loving God of grace is also a holy God of justice?

How would these stories have been different if those involved had a healthy fear of the Lord?

Read: Psalm 111:10; Proverbs 1:7; Proverbs 14:27; Acts 9:31; Acts 19:17. What do these verses have to say about the fear of the Lord?

In the chapter, several examples were given showing how fear is a great gift from the Lord. Can you think of examples where a healthy fear of something kept you safe?

Similarly, how does a healthy fear of the Lord and His consequences keep us safe?

Chapter 3 finishes by noting that a true understanding of God makes us think twice before sinning. Yet, at the same time, such an understanding also encourages running to Him when we do sin. Why is this true?

Applications Questions

Our view of God is greatly shaped by how we were raised and by the type of parents we had. With that in mind, how has your view of God been shaped by your parents/upbringing?

None of us grew up with perfect parents. If your view of God has been skewed by your parents, what can help you develop a true understanding of God's love, grace, justice, and truth?

How do you think your life would be different if you feared the Lord enough to avoid the things that displeased Him, yet understood the depths of His love enough to run to Him when you failed?

Close in Prayer

STUDY QUESTIONS
Porn

Ice Breakers
Before reading Chapter 4, if someone had asked you to list epidemics in America, would have you mentioned pornography?

Before reading Chapter 4, how big of a problem did you think porn addiction was in our nation?

What do you think about this problem now?

Chapter Study
How shocking did you find the statistics at the start of the chapter?

Which statistic(s) in particular did you find most troubling? Why?

According to much of the recent research discussed in the chapter, in what ways is an addiction to pornography just as potent (if not more so) than an addiction to heroin or cocaine?

1 Corinthians 6:18 plainly commands, *flee from sexual immorality. All other sins a person commits are outside the body, but whoever sins sexually, sins against their own body.* Thinking through the stages of the Character Formation Formula, how does the sexual sin of porn viewing literally change a person's character?

Read: Ephesians 5:3 and Colossians 3:5. Understanding how the viewing of pornography effects a person's mind and character, explain why God uses such strong language in regards to how we should handle sexual sin:

The word used for *sexuality immorality* in 1 Corinthians 6:18; Ephesians 5:3; and Colossians 3:5 is the Greek word *porneia* (which is where we get our English word for *pornography*). This word is used a total of twenty-five times in the New Testament, showing up in eleven different books. Meanwhile, "love one another" is used fifteen times in the New Testament, showing up in eight different books. What should this tell you about God's concern for the sexual purity of His people?

Applications Questions

In Chapter 4, we read that "a recent report by the Barna Group found that sixty-four percent of youth pastors, and fifty-seven percent of pastors, struggle with porn addiction. Meanwhile, seven out of ten lay leaders view pornography at least once a week, while sixty percent of Christian men and thirty percent of Christian women claim addiction to it. Of the 10,000 calls, emails, and letters Focus on the Family receives daily, porn represents the number one incoming request for help. *New Man* magazine's most frequent request from readers is to refer them to a service or a ministry that can help them with their sexual temptation." These are all troubling facts. However, only seven percent of churches have a program in place to deal with this issue. Does your church have a ministry in place to deal with addiction to pornography? If not, what should you do about this?

When it comes to your own life and home, do you have filters on all internet connected devices that you (and your children) use? If not, when will you put those filters in place?

What boundaries do you need to put in place in your home and in your life to greatly reduce the likelihood of porn grabbing a foothold in your family?

Close in Prayer

Need Help with a Porn Addiction? Use the following:
https://www.xxxchurch.com/
https://fightthenewdrug.org/get-help/
http://www.purelifeministries.org/

STUDY QUESTIONS
Entertainment Standards

Ice Breakers
What is the worst tasting food you have ever eaten?

How would you react if you detected a whiff of feces in a food you were about to ingest? How likely is it that you would choose to eat around the sullied portion?

Chapter Study
In the opening story, how does the father connect poo in brownies with "poo" in entertainment?

Why do you think people are more protective of their stomachs than their hearts and minds?

Read: Proverbs 4:23; Mark 7:19-22; Luke 6:45...What do these Scripture references have to say about the importance of our hearts and minds?

What are the stages of the Character Formation Formula?

In Chapter 5, you read, "You can take it to the bank that if what is in your heart determines the course of your life, then Satan is going to try to get whatever he can in there. Of course, he knows he would never attract us with things that are dull and boring. No, instead, he makes it all seem good by surrounding it with big budget Hollywood special effects, a funny script, great graphics, a catchy tune, etc. It's really no different than when Eve took the apple because the devil made it look *so pleasing to the eye*" (See Genesis 3:6). With this in mind, how has Satan used the blind spot of entertainment standards to effect the character of our culture?

In this chapter, the example was given of a "pervert" peering through your window screen in the hopes of seeing nudity. How is that situation really no different from the times we do the same with TV, computer, and movie screens?

Read: Colossians 3:1-4. Many say that content issues in entertainment are really no big deal because it all portrays "real life." However, according to Colossians 3, where is real life found?

How might certain entertainment choices actually work against us experiencing the fullness of Christ's reality, as well as the reality of what He desires to accomplish in and through us?

Application Questions
At one time, Hollywood used the Hays Code to regulate content. In the 1960s, this code was abandoned, and we have seen the results. However, Christians still have a code—it's called the Bible. Do you use that Code to govern your (and your family's) entertainment choices? Why or why not?

At the end of Chapter 5, we looked at God's standards for sexuality, foul language, blasphemy, violence, and the use of our time. Take a look at the verses below and determine if your life, and entertainment, choices are made in obedience to Scripture. If not, evaluate what might need to change.

Sexuality: Matthew 5:28-29; 1 Corinthians 6:18; Colossians 3:5; Ephesians 5:3

Foul Language: Ephesians 4:29; Ephesians 5:4; Colossians 3:8

Blasphemy: Exodus 20:7; Psalm 34:3; Psalm 69:30

Violence: Psalm 11:5; Isaiah 26:3; Philippians 4:7-8

Time: Psalm 90:12; Psalm 39:5; Ephesians 5:15-16; James 4:14

What "entertainment" changes should you make in your home so that it is a safe harbor, protecting those who enter from the negative effects of the culture?

Close in Prayer

STUDY QUESTIONS
The Need for Transformation

Ice Breakers

Can you think of a time in your life when you transitioned from one status to another? (I.e. single to in a relationship, engaged to married; unemployed to employed, childless to parent, being on summer vacation to student, etc.) What changes needed to occur in your life because of this transition?

Did you consult a rulebook or guidebook to determine what changes needed to be made, or did you make these changes naturally because you maturely understood that your change in status required it?

Chapter Study

Read: 2 Corinthians 5:15-17. When we become Christians, there is a change in our status. What is that change?

In Chapter 6, we read, "Being a Christian is much more than not being a sinner. Christianity is about grabbing hold of a new identity. We were once people outside of a relationship with the God of the universe, but now we are in a relationship with Him. Such a radical relationship change requires a radical lifestyle change." What are some things that go into that "radical lifestyle change"?

In the chapter, we also read, "Our new life in Christ requires a new focus--a focus on Him, on the things that please Him, and on the things that will help us live our lives as examples for a watching world." What are some things you can invest in that will encourage this change of focus?

Read: 1 Peter 4:1-5. In these verses, how do we see Peter calling us to a change in focus because of our status change?

In these verses, what does Peter say about how our unsaved friends, and really the culture in general, might react when we seek to pursue transformation?

How have your friends and family been an encouragement to your transformation process? How have they been a detriment?

Application Questions
Read: Romans 6:1-5; 12-13. What parts of your old life (sins, destructive habits, bad influences, etc.) have you yet to leave behind as you seek to grab hold of new life in Christ?

Near the end of the chapter, we read, "A ticket to heaven is not the goal, transformation is." With this in mind, how are you doing with the following?

- Daily Bible study

- Regular times of prayer throughout the day

- Gathering weekly in a small group

- Sundays in church

- Serving in a ministry

- Surrounding yourself with people who pursue Christ wholeheartedly

Who can hold you accountable to invest fully in the above?

Close in Prayer

STUDY QUESTIONS
Hell

Ice Breakers

Do you think the average person in our culture believes in the biblical reality of Hell? Why or why not?

Do you think the average Christian in our culture believes in the biblical reality of Hell? Why or why not?

What are your thoughts?

Chapter Study

In the Bible, no one speaks more on the topic of Hell than Jesus. In fact, as we discussed in Chapter 7, He spends more time warning people about the reality of Hell than He does comforting people with the reality of Heaven. Looking at the following verses, what does Jesus say about Hell?

Matthew 5:22

Matthew 7:13

Matthew 8:12

Matthew 10:28

Matthew 13:49-50

Every day, over 153,000 people die around the world. Breaking that down, close to 6,400 die every hour. That equals nearly 107 a minute (or almost two people every second). Combining those statistics with the reality of a Christ-less eternity, what should we as Christians be doing?

Read: Matthew 25:31-46. In the chapter, you were asked to imagine what it will be like to stand before the Lord on the day to end all days, to stand with those on the right and hear the God of the universe invite you to spend eternity with Him in paradise. You were then also asked to imagine seeing people you know over on the left and to think about seeing their horrified faces when Jesus tells them where they are going. What will that be like?

If you started living each day as though Christ were coming back tomorrow, would that change how you are currently living your life? Why or why not?

How should believing in the reality of Hell, along with understanding Christ could return at any moment, change how we use our time, the conversations we have, and the way we interact with those around us?

Application Steps

On a card, write down the names of at least five unsaved people that you have regular contact with:

Pray for those people right now, asking the Lord to open them up to His truth and to give you opportunities to share the Good News. Commit now to praying a similar prayer *every* day.

Set up a time to meet with at least one of those people this week.

Close in Prayer

STUDY QUESTIONS
The Spiritual Battle

Ice Breakers

If you knew that a military war was imminent and you could be called to battle, what would you do to prepare?

Since we are in a spiritual war, how important is it that we do all that is possible to be spiritually prepared for battle?

Chapter Study

How aware were you of the spiritual battle underway in our culture before reading this chapter?

What thoughts crossed your mind as you read through the stories in Chapter 8 of Christianity under attack?

Read: 1 Peter 5:8-9; Ephesians 6:10-12. Knowing that the devil is actively working to destroy Christianity and our culture, how strongly are you standing against him? In what areas are you doing well? Which areas need work?

In the chapter, we saw how the devil has historically schemed for thousands of years to get God's people to compromise, and how he is certainly doing likewise in our own culture today. In the book *UnChristian* the Christian Research Group— Barna "found that [in 28] lifestyle activities, born-again Christians were *statistically equivalent* to those of non-born agains. When asked to identify their activities over the last thirty days, born again believers were *just as likely* to gamble, visit a pornographic website, take something that didn't belong to them, consult a psychic, fight or abuse someone, consume enough alcohol to be legally drunk, to use illegal, nonprescription drugs, to lie, to get back at someone, and to have said mean things behind someone else's back" (emphasis mine). Based on these facts, how successful has the devil's war strategy been on our culture? How successful has this strategy been on you personally?

Read: Revelation 2:6, 14-16. In these verses, we see that Jesus *hates* compromise. Why is that so?

Former Navy Seal, Admiral McRaven, challenged University of Texas students to never *ring the bell*. In the chapter, this was likened to never giving into Satan's battle plan and compromising. If you answered above that the devil's war strategy has been successful on you, what must you do about this to ensure that you never ring the bell again?

How can Martin Luther's example from April, 1521 be an example for us today?

Read: Ephesians 6:13-18. The key to fighting the good fight is to put on the Armor of God and refuse to compromise. What components make up this armor?

Application Questions
Let's finish by looking intently at the Armor of God to determine how well each piece is being utilized in our lives.

The Belt of Truth: A belt might simply be seen as a fashion accessory today. However, to a Roman soldier, it was an integral and central part of their uniform. The base of the breast plate would be fastened to the belt to keep it from sliding while in battle. Further, the sword was connected to the belt, as well as several pouches containing food rations, salt for wounds, and more. Likewise, an integral and central component to a Christian's success in battle is staying anchored to the truth of God's Word. This anchor keeps us moored to our Commanding Officer and aware of His instructions. With this in mind, are you consistently reading and studying the Bible so that *[you] won't be tossed and blown about by every wind of new teaching. [And you] will not be influenced when people try to trick [you] with lies so clever they sound like the truth* (Ephesians 4:14)?

Application idea: Find a Bible study plan to go through, purchase devotional books through my website at www.markjmusser.com, or search online devotionals from

155

evangelical sources. Find ways to stay anchored to God's absolute truth.

Breastplate of Righteousness: For Roman warriors in Bible times, the metal breastplate protected most of the vital organs (particularly the heart) from blows by clubs, swords, maces, and more. For the Christian, our breastplate is a steadfast desire for righteousness, refusing to allow the devil to get at our heart—with lies, through entertainment choices, in compromise, etc. With this in mind, how well are you following Solomon's words in Proverbs 4:23, *above all else, guard your heart, for it determines the course of your life*?

Application idea: Review the last seven days. Go through your thought-life, your entertainment choices, your purchases, your word choices, your attitudes, your conversation with friends, the time you spent in kingdom building pursuits vs selfish pursuits, etc. After going through these things, ask yourself, "What might need to change?"

Shoes of Peace: We often picture Roman soldiers traveling around in thong-sandals. That, however, was not the footwear of your typical Roman fighter. A typical soldier's shoes were laced all the way up to the knee, so that they would never come off in battle. Moreover, the thick leather sole of the sandal would be studded with hobnails, creating the ancient equivalent of cleats! This gave the soldier solid footing to best stand his ground while in combat. Today, in our spiritual battle, the shoes of peace represent a solid understanding that God is on the throne and He *will* win the victory. Such knowledge keeps us surrounded in peace, as the devil throws doubt and despair and discouragement our way. Without the solid footing of knowing God is in complete control and enables our victory, it would be very easy to fall back and give up ground. With this in mind, are you living every day in the assurance that God is in control?

Application idea: Think through how you handle life when the devil assails with doubts, despair, and discouragement. Where do you run? Is it to God or to something else? If it is something else, you will need to repent of this and work to change.

Shield of Faith: Many movies depicting ancient armies show soldiers battling with relatively small, circular shields. That was not the kind of shield a Roman soldier used, however. A Roman shield was more than two feet wide and as much as four feet tall. In fact, when the Romans attacked Gaul (modern day France), the Gauls mocked them for "bringing a door to war." Nevertheless, it was so broad and effective that hardly an arrow or sword could pierce it. Understand, in this spiritual battle we are in, Satan is indeed attacking. Since that is the case, we need a faith that is deep and wide, a faith that can deflect anything the devil might throw at us. With this mind, what "faith building" exercises are you doing each day?

Application idea: As you did above, think through the past week. However, this time review how much time you spent in Scripture, in prayer, gathering with likeminded believers, and serving in a ministry. How much faith-building occurred over your last seven days? Where might you need to improve? Spiritual muscle is like physical muscle. Neither grow by accident. You must be intentional to grow in strength.

The Helmet of Salvation: The helmet of a Roman soldier,

known as a galea, is an impressive testimony to ancient craftsmanship. It not only was designed to cover the skull, but also had thick metal plates which protected the cheek and jaw bones, the back of the neck, and the forehead. Certainly, a strong blow to the head could incapacitate any soldier making him an easy target. Likewise, the devil desires to target our minds (much like he does our hearts). If he can get us to doubt our salvation, the necessity of salvation, the reality of Hell, the importance of obeying Scripture, and more, he is well on his way to incapacitating us. With this in mind, how have you noticed the devil attacking your thought life? Where does he work to get you to second guess the truth of God's Word?

Application idea: Talk through any doubts you may have about your faith or about the truth of God's Word with your pastor or a trusted church leader. Don't allow Satan to win the battle of the mind.

The Sword of the Spirit (the Word of God): A Roman soldier's sword, or gladius, was generally light (around two pounds) and less than three feet in length. Not cumbersome, it was the ideal size and weight for inflicting quick and devastating damage. In our spiritual battle, the Word of God is our offensive weapon. It is a small but powerful weapon which enables us to quickly and decisively counteract the devil's lies, the world's lures, and temptation's guiles. To use a modern weapon analogy, each Scripture we memorize is like a bullet in a gun that we can fire back at Satan when he attacks. Of course, if we don't know the Scriptures well, Satan has no problem taking down the unarmed. With this in mind, how well do you know the Scriptures? How many verses do you have memorized?

Application idea: Develop a plan where you memorize a verse or two a week. Moreover, don't just read the Bible, study it. There are many online tools to help you do just that.

Close in Prayer

APPENDIX

Blind Spot -- Sin
1. Psalm 5:5
2. Psalm 11:5
3. Jeremiah 44:4
4. Galatians 6:7-8
5. Luke 6:12
6. Luke 4:42
7. Matthew 27:46
8. John 5:14
9. John 8:11
10. 1 Corinthians 15:34
11. 1 John 2:4-6
12. Isaiah 53:10
13. Luke 6:46-49
14. John 14:15
15. John 15:14
16. John 14:23-24
17. Genesis 6:5-6

Blind Spot – Gossip
1. Price, Steven D *1001 Dumbest Things Ever Said* Lyons Press, April 1, 2005
2. http://www.sermonillustrations.com/a-z/g/gossip.htm
3. Proverbs 18:20-21
4. James 3:1-6
5. https://www.theatlantic.com/health/archive/2012/04/what-kinds-of-happy-couples-eventually-get-divorced/255922/
6. Proverbs 16:27-28
7. Proverbs 26:22

Blind Spot -- The Fear of the Lord
1. "This is a Brain on Adolescence" Temple Review
2. Ingram, Chip, Course Workbook: "Effect Parenting in a Defective World: How to Raise Kids Who Stand Out from the Crowd" www.walkthru.org
3. Ingram, Chip "How to Discipline Your Child Effectively" Living on the Edge Atlanta, GA, 2003.
4. "Teens and alcohol study: Parenting style can prevent binge drinking" news.byu.edu
5. Santrock, J.W. A topical approach to life-span development, third Ed. New York: McGraw-Hill 2007.
6. "Grace Wins" Matthew West, Sparrow Records, 2015
7. John 4:8; 4:16; Psalm 99:9; Isaiah 6:3; Revelation 4:8
8. Ephesians 5:3; Colossians 3:5
9. www.fightthenewdrug.org
10. IBID
11. IBID
12. IBID

Blind Spot – Porn
1. Ropelato, Jerry, "Internet Pornography Statistics" www.toptenreviews.com
2. http://www.foxnews.com/tech/2017/12/19/net-neutralitys-impact-on-free-porn-could-be-significant-experts-say.html
3. https://fightthenewdrug.org/most-popular-porn-genre-search-of-2016/
4. https://www.webroot.com/us/en/home/resources/tips/digital-family-life/internet-pornography-by-the-numbers
5. "Teens Forge Forward with the Internet and Other New Technologies," www.pewtrusts.org July 29, 2005

6. Ropelato, Jerry, "Internet Pornography Statistics" www.toptenreviews.com
7. IBID
8. "Kids Top 100 Searches of 2009" onlinefamilyinfo.norton.com
9. Bruin, Gordon S. "Understanding Why Pornography Addiction is a Brain Disease" www.hubpages.com
10. http://www.covenanteyes.com/2014/02/28/hypofrontality/
11. https://www.ncbi.nlm.nih.gov/pmc/articles/PMC4600144/
12. https://fightthenewdrug.org/why-consuming-porn-is-an-escalating-behavior/
13. https://fightthenewdrug.org/how-consuming-porn-can-lead-to-violence/
14. Kelly, David "Yupaica teens cited for 'sexting' nude photos of classmates" www.latimes.com April 15, 2010
15. http://www.covenanteyes.com/2016/01/19/what-are-the-most-up-to-date-stats-on-pornography/.
16. http://www.transparentministries.org/porn-stats/

Blind Spot – Entertainment Standards

1. http://www.faithandfire.org/stories/Stories89.html
2. Proverbs 4:23
3. Luke 6:45
4. Proverbs 27:19
5. Colossians 3:5
6. Ephesians 5:3
7. 1 Corinthians 6:18
8. Genesis 3:6
9. Colossians 3:1-4
10. Philippians 4:8
11. Matthew 5:29
12. 1 John 3:3

13. 1 Timothy 4:12
14. Colossians 3:8
15. Ephesians 5:4
16. Ephesians 4:29
17. https://www.cbsnews.com/news/profanity-laced-tv-video-games-tied-to-cursing-aggression/
18. Exodus 20:7
19. Psalm 34:3
20. Psalm 69:30
21. "Research on the Effects of Media Violence" www.media-awareness.ca
22. IBID
23. American Academy of Pediatrics Policy Statement, Volume 95, Number 6 - June 1995
24. Psalm 90:12
25. Psalm 39:5
26. James 4:14
27. http://www.cnn.com/2016/06/30/health/americans-screen-time-nielsen/index.html
28. https://www.statista.com/statistics/276683/media-use-in-the-us/

Blind Spot -- Transformation
1. Romans 3:23
2. 2 Corinthians 5:15,17
3. Revelation 19:7; 21:2; 21:9
4. Colossians 3:1-4
5. Jeremiah 2:13
6. Jeremiah 2:18
7. Romans 6:1-5; 12,13; Holy Bible, New International Reader's Version® Copyright © 1995, 1996, 1998 by Biblica
8. https://ethanrenoe.com/2017/12/06/the-dumbing-down-of-christianity/
9. Romans 12:2a

10. Hebrews 5:12-14

Blind Spot – Hell
1. https://www.gotquestions.org/does-hell-exist.html
2. IBID
3. Matthew 5:22
4. Matthew 5:29
5. Matthew 7:13
6. Matthew 10:28
7. Matthew 8:12
8. Matthew 13:42
9. Matthew 13:49-50
10. See Matthew 25:31-46

Blind Spot – The Spiritual Battle
1. "Christian group now allowed to distribute fliers at Penn. School," www.alliancedefensefund.org, January 27, 2009.
2. "ACLJ Files Religious Discrimination Suit against Colorado School District for Denying Students Permission to Form Bible Club at School" www.aclj.org January 6, 2003.
3. "Conn. Town Can't Hold Graduations in Church, Judge Rules" www.foxnews.com, May 31, 2010.
4. Coulter, Ann, "It's the winter solstice, Charlie Brown!" www.townhall.com September 25, 2003.
5. Steele, Mandy. "Christmas book banned from class: Parents sue district after teacher censors 2nd-grader's story." www.wnd.com, July 30, 2002.
6. "Student barred from singing "Awesome God" www.wnd.com May 27, 2005
7. The Rutherford Institute newsletter, March, 1995
8. Cal Thomas, "Russia Learned What America Has Scorned," AFA Journal, Feb. 1993.

9. http://faithandthelaw.wordpress.com/2010/05/page/12/

10. "Illinois Moment of Silence in Schools Ruled Unconstitutional," www.foxnews.com, January 22, 2009.

11. Revelation 2:14-15

12. *Life Application Study Bible*, Tyndale House Publishers Inc, 2nd Edition, October, 2004

13. Kinnaman, David; *unChristian: What a New Generation Really Thinks about Christianity…and Why It Matters*, Baker Books, April 2012

14. Ephesians 6:13,14a

15. Badash, David; "Bill Maher: 'The Culture War Is Over And We Won!'" May 24, 2014

16. https://www.cbssports.com/nfl/news/dolphins-fine-and-suspend-db-don-jones-for-anti-michael-sam-tweet/

17. https://www.youtube.com/watch?v=pxBQLFLei70

18. Bunyon, John; The Pilgrim's Progress, Moody Publishers, October 1, 2007

Epilogue

1. 1 Corinthians 2:16

2. Romans 12:2

3. 2 Corinthians 10:5

4. Galatians 2:20